To Do or NOT to Do: Shakespeare Gone Astray! (in 3D)

Or... Out, Vile Jelly-filled Donut!

A FULL-LENGTH PLAY
by Katherine Tartaglia Dumont

Copyright © 2012 Katherine Tartaglia Dumont
All rights reserved.
ISBN-10: 0615951694
ISBN-13: 978-0615951690

To Do or NOT to Do: Shakespeare Gone Astray! (in 3D)
Copyright 2012 Katherine Tartaglia Dumont

ALL RIGHTS RESERVED

Performance Rights: This play is the property of the author. To obtain performance rights to this play visit www.soggynoodle.com and follow the directions therein. Or you can contact the author directly: cold_porridge@msn.com Unauthorized performances are villainous and will result in disaster and disgrace. For performance-related questions, the author may be contacted through aforementioned website or e-mail address.

Photocopying: Or otherwise duplicating this book is prohibited. Unauthorized copying or redistribution in any format is thievery, and may you choke on your haggis.

Bulk orders: For cast sets of the play at a reduced cost, go to www.soggynoodle.com.

Author credit: Any group or individual producing this play is required to accredit the author in any publication relating to the play, including performance programs, advertising, etc. The name of the author may not be obliterated, abbreviated or otherwise altered.

Cover art credit: Copyright 2012 Nadia Herman. Permission to use cover art must be obtained from the artist, who will charge a small fee for her design. For information, contact: hermanspanama@gmail.com.

Permission to use musical works: There are musical works referenced in this play. Performance rights to this play do not extend to rights to perform referenced musical recordings/compositions.

Photo credit: Katherine T. Dumont—images of actors used with permission.

Alterations: The author, having written this play to meet the needs of her cast, certainly understands and approves if a director needs to make adaptations, within reason, to meet the needs of his/her cast. Narrators 1 and 3 were written specifically for guys and Narrator 2 for a girl—it would not work well to cast them otherwise. But the rest of the characters could be cast cross-gendered as needed. Have fun with it!

Cast: Ideally about 20 actors, but could accommodate up to 40, approximately half male half female. Perhaps this play could be performed with as few as 10 insanely talented and energetic actors. (If you try it, the author would like to know how it went!) For ideas on how to cast for about 20 actors, see original cast list at the end of book.

Length: Approximately 110-125 minutes, depending on efficiency of actors, music, scene changes, amount of haggis consumed, etc.

Staging: The sets for this play could be simple or elaborate, depending on budget. A Globe Theater façade is a nice touch, to set the scene, and a balcony of some sort is needed.

Costuming: Garb for this production may be as elaborate or ridiculous as your budget and talents allow. For a photo gallery of costuming from original production, visit www.soggynoodle.com and go to the *Vile Jelly 2012* page.

CONTENTS

Acknowledgments	1
Cast List	2
Act 1	5
Act 2	44
Original Cast List	84
Pseudo-Shakespearean Insults	85
Body Parts Referenced	86
Useful Props by Scene	87
Notes	90

ACKNOWLEDGMENTS

The author would like to thank her clever and nerdy husband and boys, without whom there would be no stupid *Star Wars* references in this traditional Shakespearean play. Additionally, they are lifesavers any time she encounters technical difficulties, which is quite often.

And she would like to recognize her talented troupe of young actors who were willing to "get out of their comfort zones" and give this production a test run. They are always full of surprises and imaginative ideas!

Katherine T. Dumont

CAST:

(Narrators 1, 2, and 3 should be cast as specified for gender. For the rest, cast however it pleases you! Cross-dressing is encouraged!)

N1/Macbuff (male)
N2/Ophelia (female)
N3/Weird Sisters/Luke (male)
Annie/Puck
Han-Romeo
Obi/Friar Obi
JuLeia
Captain Undergarments /Bottom
Minstrel/Coriolanus
Hamlet
Pambic Boy
Queen Elizabeth/Titania
Column 1
Column 2
Timon
Jeweler
Poet
Painter
Ventidius
Lucilius
Girlfriend
Apemantus
Volumnia
Valeria
Duke Orsino
Viola
Valentine/Malvolio
Olivia
Sebastian
Banquo, etc.
Lady Macbeth

To Do or NOT to Do...

Helena
Hermia
Lymetrius
Oberon
Butt Custodian
King Lear
Goneril
Regan
Cordelia
Paramedic
Claudius
Gertrude
Ghost/Vader voice (should be N1)
Polonius (could be N3)
Laertes
Yoda-logue
Sampson
Abraham
Wookiee arms and sounds
Henry 8th (could be Captain Undergarments)

Katherine T. Dumont

AUTHOR'S INTRO:

　　This play was written for an experienced troupe of pre-teen and teen actors after collecting their suggestions about what they wanted in their next play. They wanted comedy, they wanted Shakespeare, and yes, they wanted plenty of GIRL PARTS! It therefore made the most sense to create a "collage" play to give each actor the opportunity to shine! Although this play is, as a whole, a comedy, it contains plenty of opportunity for serious moments, particularly in the monologues if you choose to give them the weight they deserve.

To Do or NOT to Do: Shakespeare Gone Astray! (in 3D)
by Katherine Tartaglia Dumont

ACT 1

Two actors enter with a basket full of papers.

N1   Well, the ballots are in. We had the actors give suggestions for tonight's play. The director was having a brain freeze.

N2   Let's see what they say. *(opens one)* Yes! *The Hunger Games!* *(aims a pretend arrow at the audience)* Plenty of violence *and* two love interests!

N3   *(entering)* Nah—there's a movie version of that. We like to beat the movie directors to it, like we did with the *Hobbit*. Ha Ha—slow poke, Peter Jackson!

N1   *(reminiscing)* There and back again. *That* was an awesome adventure. Remember when you. . . *(miming something embarrassing)*

N3   *(cutting him off, looking embarrassed)* Next? *(looking over N2's shoulder)*

N2   Biffy the Vampire Slayer

N3   Buffy.

N2   No, it says Biffy. *(showing him)*

N1   *(grabs cape, inserts fangs, and goes over to N2)* I vant to suck your blood.

N3   No, he'd ruin it.

N2   Besides, everybody's doing vampire or zombie plays.

(Orphan Annie girl actor enters, sweeping nonchalantly—she drops a suggestion into the basket from behind the narrators while they face forward.)

N2   *(pulls out next one)* Annie?

(Annie sprints downstage and breaks into song.)

Annie   *(sings with over the top expression)* "Oh, the sun'll come out to. . ."

N3 Sorry, we don't do musicals. *(pointing at N1 and plugging ears)* Try the Fine Arts' Guild. *(insert your own rival theater company or school)*

Annie *(N1 and N3 pick her up, legs kicking, and escort her off stage as she continues to sing.)* "bet your bottom. . . *(reappearing in the balcony!)* there'll be. . ." *(N1 and N3 threaten her with hand signals, and she leaves.)*

N2 *(continues Annie song quietly to herself—then stops when other two notice)* Sorry, it's catchy. Next, *(opening another)* Robin Hood.

N1 *(sarcastically)* Well, we do like wearing tights and tunics.

N2 But there are only two girl parts, and they are both weak and subservient. Besides, some of us are getting tired of sporting mustaches.

N3 *(sticking a mustache on her)* Oh, but they look so good on you!

N1 *(pulls out next suggestion)* Shrek. Uh, I think we're out of green face paint. Plus, there are copyright issues with that one.

N2 Let's not go *there*. *(pulls out next and reads carefully)* Lysistrata.

N1 Sounds Greek to me. I'm not wearing a sheet.

N3 Sounds like a cross between a mouth wash and a Danish pastry to *me*. What *else* is there? *(pulls out an obvious one folded into the shape of a pod racer and hands it to her with a big, hopeful smile—gives thumbs-up cue to sound guy)*

N2 Star Wars?

(Star Wars theme comes on, and Han Solo enters—N3 directs him into a freeze.)

N2 *(to N3)* I take it this was your idea.

N3 Yes, young Padawan.

N1 Hey, I suggested it, too!

(whips out Darth Vader costume and light saber) We meet again at last. The theater is now complete. When I left you, I was but the stagehand. I am the director now.

To Do or NOT to Do...

Obi *(Obi enters)* Only a director of Evil, Darth. *(duel)* If you smite me down, I shall become more potent than you can possibly envision.

Han *(unfreezes)* Damn idiot, I totally knew you were gonna say that.

Obi Who is more idiotic, the idiot or the idiot who follows him?

Han Look, I've been in a lot of plays and seen a lot of scenes, but I've never seen anything to make me believe in some all-mighty force.

N3/Luke *(putting on Luke costume)* The force?

Obi The force is an energy field created by all breathing actors. It surrounds us and penetrates us. It binds the theater together. You must learn the ways of the force if you are to perform with us.

N3/Luke Sweet. I could learn the ways of the force with you and Yoda, find out that Darth Vader's my dad, nearly get killed by him, try to save him and almost kill him, and then watch someone else kill him instead. But it all works out in the end.

N2 Enough! It's not happening, Luke.

JuLeia *(as she enters)* There aren't enough girl parts.

Obi *(goes behind JuLeia, puts burger buns on her head and says, temptingly)* There's a princess...

Han *(looking at N2)* and Jabba the Hut's wife!

N2 *(sarcastically)* Oh yes, every girl's dream part.

Luke&Han *(make blasting noises at each other)* pshew pshew pshew pshew

JuLeia Why don't you guys go back to Tatooine or LegoLand or whatever stupid planet you came from?

Han *(explaining details)* First, we are on Tatooine and then the Death Star and the fourth moon of Yavin and finally we end up...

JuLeia Where do you get your illusions, blaster brains?

N3/Luke *(excited)* Yeah, yeah—you're gettin' it!

N2&JuLeia *(together)* It's not happening.

(The four boys look at each other conspiratorially and smile.)

Obi   Heh heh, okay. Whatever you say.

Han   But you haven't even seen our Wookiee! *(Obi nudges him to shut up.)*

JuLeia   Back to your spaceships, stargeeks.

(Han and Obi leave, speaking Star Wars as they go—JuLeia stays on stage but sits down on the side somewhere and watches.)

Han   Han shoot first, or later?

Obi   First, man. Definitely first. *(mimes shooting laser)*

N3/Luke   *(to audience)* Han or Luke?

N2   *(dragging N3 away from audience)*   Back to the drawing board, Luke. I mean, drawing bucket. I mean, (N3's real name). *(rolls her eyes and pulls out another idea)* Snow White.

N3   *(in a girly voice, flitting about)* Oh yes! Fetch me my apples! *(grabs apples from basket and starts to put them in his shirt)*

N1   *(takes apples from N3)* Been there, done that. We don't need to see *them* apples again.

N2   For sure. *(cringing and shaking head)*

N3   You're right. It's never a good idea to do the same play twice. It's like. . . eating a bowl of pudding and then throwing it up and eating it again. Loses its appeal.

N2   Gross. You've ruined pudding for me for life.

(N1 makes a note of this and tries to nonchalantly make a pass at her.)

N1   So, what kinds of desserts *do* you like?

N2   *(ignoring him, pulls out next vote)* Captain Undergarments?

N3   Who put that in th. . .

(Actor dressed ridiculously as Captain Undergarments runs in and poses.)

To Do or NOT to Do...

Captain U Bring me my purple porta-potty, and let's go visit the gas giants! Has anyone seen my bionic gerbil? *(pulls out stuffed rodent)* Oh, here you are! Tr-la-laaaa!

N1 Well, I think that answers that question. Have you ever noticed that most super heroes tend to wear their underwear on the outside of their pants?

N3 Been there, done that.

(all look at him—N1 and N2 with disgust, CU with brotherly bonding)

N2 Eww—you've ruined super heroes for me for life! I think we can move on from puke and toilets. We need something more mature. I *am* a teenager, you know.

N1 *(in a very grown up voice, to impress N2)* Yes, we need something more mature. I myself am a teenage...

N3 *(interrupting)* Mutant Ninja Turtle

N1 *(proudly)* young adult... *and* moving on to the next suggestion:

N2 Shakespeare. Well, that's a little vague. But it has potential for maturity.

N3 *(excited and clapping)* Oh yes—*great* potential! *(scheming in his head)*

N1 Well, he's not my least unfavorite playwright. But there are so many plays to choose from, like over 100!

N3 I think it's closer to 37, give or take a few, depending on your alliances.

N2 Which one *will* we do?

N3 Nice pun—he would have liked that.

N1 *I* am ready to be more mature. But do you think we really know enough to pull off the BIG GUY?

N3 I know a bit of Shakespeare, at least as much as *that* guy, I'll bet. *(pointing to someone in audience)*

N1 Really? Prove it.

N3 Alright—be right back.

(N3 cues the sound guy to play Renaissance music—then he heads backstage to change into Shakespearean attire: puffy

shorts, tunic, tights, ridiculous looking ruff, props, etc. Meanwhile, N1 and N2 must kill time with ad lib while they await his return. First they might dance a little to the music. Then they could question his intentions or crack jokes about him: "Do you think he really knows any Shakespeare?" "He is probably putting on tights." "What in the world is he doing back there?" "Sorry, folks." *Then they should head into the audience to find out how much they know about Shakespeare, starting with "that guy." They could see how many plays the audience can name.*

N3 *(yelling from backstage)* I come, anon!

(N1 and N2 return to stage with questioning looks and more ad lib comments—looks of concern when N3 returns in his new get-up and does his pre-monologue stretching.)

JuLeia Why is he wearing a coffee filter around his neck?

N1 Well, get on with it.

(Any monologue could be used here, as long as it is obscure and not used later on in the play. For the monologue below, N3 could place hats on N1, N2, and JuLeia to indicate that they are Bardolph, Pistol, and Nym—they should appear skeptical and annoyed!)

N3/BOY As young as I am, I have observed these three swashers. I am boy to all three; but all three, though they would serve me, could not be man to me; for indeed three such antics do not amount to a man. For Bardolph, he is white-livered and red-faced; by the means whereof 'a faces it out, but fights not. For Pistol, he hath a killing tongue and a quiet sword; by the means whereof 'a breaks word and keeps whole weapons. For Nym, he hath heard that men of few words are the best men, and therefore he scorns to say his prayers; but his few bad words are matched with as few good deeds, for 'a never broke any man's head but his own, and that was against a post when he was drunk. They will steal anything, and call it purchase. Bardolph stole a lute-case, bore it twelve leagues, and sold it for three halfpence. Nym and Bardolph are sworn brothers in filching, and in Calais they stole a fire-shovel. I knew by that piece of service the men would carry coals. They would have me as familiar with men's pockets as their gloves or handkerchers; which makes much against my manhood. I must leave them. Their villainy goes against my weak stomach, and therefore I must cast it up. *(takes a bow and pretend pukes—perhaps into Bardolph's hat!)*

N2   *(shocked)* What was that?

N3   Boy, from *Henry V*.

N1   You just *happen* to know that?

N3   Don't *you* have a Shakespearean monologue ready, just in case? Pretty much *all* actors do.

JuLeia *(embarrassed)* Um, really?

N1   *I* don't.

N3   For shame! And you call yourselves actors!

N1   But, we—

N2   Perhaps he's right. Maybe it *would* be useful for us *all* to know more Shakespeare. . . to make us more marketable. . . as actors.

N1   It's not a bad idea.

Hamlet *(enters)* I wouldn't mind knowing something. I've always wanted to know that "to do or not to do" spiel.

N3   To *be* or not to *be*. It's all yours.

Hamlet Sweet. *(to himself as he exits)* To *BE* or not to *BE*. To *BE* or not to *BE*.

N2   So I take it we're doing *Hamlet*. One girl gets to go crazy and drown in a river while the rest of us don cod pieces?

N1   Awesome!

N2   *(to N1)* Do you even know what a cod piece is?

N1   Uh. . . some type of fishbikini?

N2   Maybe you'd better Google it.

(N1 pulls out an iPhone or similar gadget.)

N2   *(sarcastically)* I claim the one who goes batty and can't swim.

N3   No, wait a minute. Who says we have to do just one play? I think we can *have* our cake *and* eat it, too.

N1 You mean do all 37, give or take a few, of them? *(looking at audience for response)*

N2 I don't think they want to stay all month.

N1 We have to keep it under two hours. That's all we've paid for to use this place.

N3 I'll bet we can find something for *all* of our actors in that fat folio. Let's honor those suggestions and make *everyone* happy.

N2 *(skeptically)* Really? *Hunger Games?*

N3 Stories of conspiracy and revenge—let's see, that's like every comedy plus most of the tragedies and histories. And double love interests everywhere you turn as well.

N1 *(Googling)* Not just double—triple and quadruple love interests, plus twins and double twins!

N2 Biffy the Vampire . . .

N3 *(cutting her off)* Bloodthirsty women? *(holds her hands in front of her until she thinks of it)*

N2 *(looking at her hands)*—Lady Macb. . .

N3 *(cutting her off)* The Scottish Play, with bonus witches. That won't be hard to cast! *(looking at JuLeia, who scowls at him)*

Annie *(Annie comes in sweeping and looking forlorn.)*

N1 *(looking at her)* Annoying characters who sweep and sing?

N3 *(goes over to her and grabs her broom and sweeps, rhythmically)* I am sent with broom before, to sweep the dust behind the door. *(hands broom back and whispers to her)*

Annie *(singing)* Can I sing it?

N1 *(singing, off key)* Of course you can sing it!

N3 *(mouths to audience)* See what I mean?

Annie *(singing to the tune of "Tomorrow")* I love ya, Will Shakespeare! *(They shoo her off to get ready.)*

N2 *(reading through list)* Tights and tunics.

N3 Check.

N2 Funny Greek names?

N1 *(Googling more)* Apemantus and Ventidius in *Timon of Athens*, check.

N2 Dueling.

N1&N3 *(grab a light saber and a sword and duel)* Duh.

N2 Violence and murder?

N3 Everywhere.

N1 Wookies?

N3 I know there's a big, hairy beast in there somewhere.

N1 *Shrek?*

N3 Fairy tale with green face paint and a talking donkey—no problemo.

N2 Teen romance—

N1 Well, there's the big one, *R and J*. Plus, weren't all lovers teenagers back then? They had a much shorter life span, so they had to get on it *[or "get it on!"]* practically out of the cradle.

N2 *(looking at the two boys)* I'm so glad *I* will have more time to wait.

N3 Yeah, it must have been like, give me a kiss. . .oh wait, let me take out my retainer. *(examines pretend retainer)* Huh—leftover curds and whey.

N2 *(disappointed)* Eew—you've ruined kisses for me for life! *(puts hand over mouth to stop from gagging while N3 pretends to toss retainer into audience)*

N1 *(seeing Captain Undergarments looking left out)* How about cracks, I mean jokes, about butts? That could be tough with all that fancy language.

N3 Are you kidding me? Will was the master of the adolescent mind. He had a whole character who was literally a butt-head. Remember good old donkey boy, Nick Bottom? Plus, there's an entire play devoted exclusively to someone's rear end! *Coriolanus!*

N2 What's that about?

N3 No idea, butt it meets our requirements.

(Minstrel wanders in, perhaps with a lute, up in the balcony.)

N1 Hey you, wandering minstrel, you are in charge of researching *Coriolanus*.

Minstrel Researching whose what?

N1 *Coriolanus.*

Minstrel That was one of my spelling words: C-O-R-I-O-L-A-N-U-S.

N3 Perfect. Get on it.

Minstrel *(leaves, spelling something rude under his breath, like* C-O-D-P-I-E-C-E*)*

N2 *(taking notes)* Well, I think we have our line-up. And this way there should be *plenty* of girl parts.

N1 *(dreaming)* Yes, *girl* parts!

N3 *(calling backstage)* Actors! *(about six actors enter— JuLeia joins them)* Here are the plays we must cover: con them in the next ten minutes while *we* waste time on stage.

N2 And while we're at it, we'll make sure *every* actor gets a monologue out of the deal. *(looking at other two)* Always good to have one on your resume.

(N3 hands out Shakespeare books to the pack of actors while N1 and N2 add Ren-garb to their attire—actors ad lib various responses as they head backstage to prepare, like "Who's King Lear?")

N1 *(still tying tunic)* So, how shall we fill this time?

N3 How about a little background to begin?

N1 You're just going to pull that out of your...

N2 Absolutely. Like he does everything else.

N3 I'll bet that between your Google habit and the collective mind of the masses out there, we've got it covered. There's not that much to know about the guy. It's not like they had Facebook back then. If we just stick to the facts, there are only about five of them. All the rest is speculation.

N2 Alright, let's try it. We'll quiz the audience, and *you* confirm their answers on Willipedia.

N3 *(to audience)* This will be one of those fill in the blank quizzes. Ready?

N2 William Shakespeare was born in the year _____ in the town of _____.

N3 He aspired to be a _____ like his _____, but instead he was really good at <u>blank</u>, <u>blank</u>, and <u>blank</u>. I need three verbs, folks! *(gets three verbs from the audience and repeats)* But instead he was really good at _____, _____, and _____. When he was a boy, Little Willy always ate _____ for supper, and. . .

N2 Okay, enough! This is starting to sound like a Mad Lib. What are you finding, (N1's name)?

N1 *(Angry Birds music or something is heard on the iphone.)* Uh. . .

N3 You know, no one really cares about the facts anyway. Why don't we just focus on the literature itself.

N1 Literature? I like math.

N2 Math? You can't be an actor if you don't *love* literature.

N1 I'm not saying I. . . it's just that I prefer math.

N3 Well, Shakespeare's writing is really all about math, is it not? He was obviously a number person.

N1&N2 *(together)* Huh?

N3 Take the iambic pentameter, for example. It's *all* patterns and counting.

N1 The pambic what? I'm taking advanced calculus, and I've never heard of that. Sounds like a disease.

N3 *(spoken with emphasis on the iambic rhythm)*
Oh yes, it's very catching you will see
how ev'ry single word must fall in line
to make the iamb fit just perfectly
in ten syllabic beats not ever nine.

N2 *(counting)* Whoa! How did you do that?

N3 *(again emphasizing iambic rhythm)*
I've read a lot of Seuss which really helps,

except that he was more an anapest:
(now emphasizing anapestic rhythm)
From the piffulous pond came the hideous sound

N2 Yes, I get it! *(finishing the rhyme)*
Of the gummy worms worming
while squirming around.

N1 You are BOTH ANA*PESTS!* Now I'm starting to see how annoying you two are if YOU ASK ME!

(N2 and N3 shaking their heads)

N2 *(with anapestic rhythm)*
No, you didn't quite get it, but started okay.

N3 It was right at your ending that things went astray. *(high five each other)*

N1 Can we just get back to Shakespeare and that iamb thing?

N3 *(more iambic rhythm)*
Oh yes, I think that would be apropos;
to get the point across we'll start real slow.

N2 Hey, we're actors—let's act it out!

N3 Great idea! You two will be the iamb.

N1 *(hopeful)* You mean, like a couple? *(leaning toward N2)*

N3 Exactly. The two of you will form the rhythm, using two "bams."

N2 *(shaking head and giving him a disgusted glare)* Uh uhh.

N3 Oh, come on. It's only for one meter.

N2 *(aside)* The longest meter of my life.

N1 *(to audience)* The greatest meter of my life!

N3 If you don't mind, I think I will direct. *(grabs stick or light saber and motions them into place—then directs)*

N2 *(tiny and quiet)* bam

N1 *(loud and extreme)* BAM!

(They practice under N3's direction until it is fluent, or they have had enough!)

N2 Alright, I think we've got it. Now how about the rest of it, the pentameter?

N1 Penta meter! I get it! Penta means five, and meter is the unit length.

N3 That's right, math geek. Now figure out how many more volunteers we will need.

N1 Well, two syllables per iamb *(toward N2)*, that's you and me, babe! And there are five of them, so a total of 10—that means eight more bodies to act out one whole line.

N3 *(to audience)* Now, don't all of you raise your hands at once.

N2 We could use some of our highly trained actors from backstage.

Pambic Boy Phew, thought you'd never ask. It's getting awfully rank back there. And there's a queen trying to boss everyone around. Says she's Good Queen Bess.

N3 That's Renaissance life for ya. Why don't you go grab three backstage cronies and you can each select your own partner from the audience.

Pambic Boy Really? *(checks out audience, smiles and waves at someone)* Be right back!

(Queen Elizabeth, covered in hideous white make-up, storms out.)

Queen Hold it! I don't remember giving approval for this business in my court.

N2 Who died and left you queen, Lady Gaga?

Queen My half sister, Mary. *(steps downstage center and royally addresses the audience)* My people, the rule of nature moves me to sorrow for my sister; the burden that has fallen upon me makes me astonished, and yet, considering I am God's creature, I will thereto yield to His grace to be the executer of His heavenly will in this office now bestowed upon me. And as I am but one being naturally considered, so shall I need you all. . . to be assistant to me, that I with my governing and you with your service may make a virtuous account to Almighty God and leave some well-being to our posterity on earth. I mean to perform all my deeds by good advice and counsel.

N1 Then here's some good advice and counsel: get off the stage! We are doing a collection of Shakespeare plays, and I don't think there's one about you.

N3 Well, actually, Queen Elizabeth would have been pretty important to our bard, and he certainly would *not* have wanted to offend her. We better make her happy. In fact, I think Will Shakespeare honored her at the end of *Henry VIII* after she died.

Queen He did? He wrote about me?

N2 If we don't let her stay, she'll probably have us beheaded.

N1 *(yelling backstage)* Add *Henry VIII* to the list!

(from backstage, singing: "I'm Henry the 8th I am. . .")

Queen *(to narrators)* Is that Falstaff guy going to be here? He's my favorite.

N1 *(yells backstage)* Somebody needs to be Falstaff!

(Obi shouts, from backstage: "Holograph?")

Queen *(settling onto a makeshift throne)* So, where were we?

N3 We were just killing time while our actors. . .

Queen Well, I'm ready now. What's first?

N2 Uh. . . *(looks at the others)*

N1 Why don't we go in chronological order—start with the Greeks.

N3 Ah, yes. Timon? Timon? *(pronounces it both ways, short i then long i)* of Athens. Only one consonant—let's assume *long* vowel sound.

Captain U *(arriving out of nowhere)* Did I hear bowel sounds?

N2 *(to N3)* Get him out of here.

N3 *(escorting Captain Undergarments out and yelling to backstage)* We need the Greeks!

(Two actors arrive, dressed as Greek columns, and situate themselves—could be accompanied by "Greek" music. After a few moments, it is obvious there is a delay with the other Greek actors.)

N1 So, where are the actors with the funny names?

To Do or NOT to Do. . .

Column 1 Timon's sheet doesn't fit.

Column 2 Ventidius and Apemantus are fighting over who gets the flat and who gets the fitted. *(or could use "top" and "bottom" instead)*

N3 *(to N1)* Kill some more time with an intro or something. I'll go check it out. *(goes backstage)*

N1 Uh. . . *(Googling)* Rarely performed, obscure, difficult, and depressing, *Timon of Athens* was originally grouped with the tragedies, but now many scholars prefer to group it with the "problem plays." *(use finger quotes)* It is about a noble and wealthy Athenian who is obsessed with being generous and giving away his money and possessions. He is therefore surrounded by "friends." *(use finger quotes)*

Queen Oh goody, here he comes.

Timon *(enters, wearing only a pillowcase)* Sorry, I gave away all my sheets, so I had to make do with this pillowcase. Oh look, here come my friends.

(enter Poet, Painter, and Jeweler, dressed in assorted sheets)

Jeweler I have a jewel here, for the Lord Timon.

Timon Oh, thank you, thank you. And here is something for you.

(hands Jeweler a big bag of gold)

Poet Shall I recite a poem for you?
"Our poesy is as a gum which oozes."

Timon How poetic! Thank you, thank you. And here is something for you. *(hands Poet a big bag of gold)*

Painter *(showing Timon a painting)* A picture sir—'tis a pretty mocking of life.

Timon *(looking at a terrible painting of himself in a pillowcase)* 'Tis! Oh, thank you, thank you. And here is something for you. *(hands Painter a big bag of gold)*

Column 1 Ventidius is in prison for not paying his bills.

Timon Imprisoned is he, say you?

Column 1 Ay, my good Lord; five talents is his debt, his means most short, creditors most strait.

Timon Well. I am not of that feather, to shake off my friend when he must need me. Here, go pay his debt and free him. *(hands Column 1 a big bag of gold)*

(Column 1 goes backstage and returns with Ventidius, who is wearing a striped prisoner sheet—Ventidius then just sits out of the way, looking like a criminal.)

Column 2 Thou hast a servant named Lucilius?

Timon I have so; what of him?

Column 2 He does not have the money to marry his girlfriend. The maid is young and fair and bred by her father at dearest cost in qualities of the best.

Timon *(calling backstage)* Come, Lucilius!

Column 1 *(to Column 2)* That's a silly name.

Lucilius *(enters, in a messed-up sheet)* Here, my Lord.

Timon Love you the maid?

Lucilius Aye, my good Lord.

Timon Here then. *(handing him three bags of gold)* This ought to cover it.

Lucilius *(excited, and running off)* Humbly I thank you, my Lord.

Timon *(calling after him)* And don't worry about coming to work tomorrow!

Lucilius *(calling back)* I won't, my Lord.

Painter *(showing another hideous painting)* Another painting, which I do beseech your Lordship to accept.

Timon Painting is welcome. *(holds up painting)* This painting is almost the natural man! *(hands Painter another bag of gold)*

Jeweler Look, my Lord, another jewel. *(hands him a common rock)*

Timon *(holding up the rock)* Oh, how exquisite! We must needs dine together. Let's have a banquet to celebrate my generosity.

Poet Generosity, generosity. The opposite of paucity.

Timon Brilliant, poet. *(hands Poet another bag of gold)*

Column 1 Uh oh. Here comes Apemantus to ruin the party. *(pronounced "Ape")*

N3   Are you sure it isn't Apemantus? *(pronounced "Appa")*

(angry ape man in sheet enters)

N2   Too late.

Timon   O, Apemantus, you are welcome to dine with us. Whither art thou going?

Ape   *(angrily)* To knock out an honest Athenian's brains.

Timon   That's a deed thou'lt die for. How dost thou like this jewel, Apemantus? *(holding up rock)* What dost thou think 'tis worth?

Ape   Not worth my thinking.

Timon   How lik'st this picture, Apemantus? *(holding up hideous painting)*

Ape   Time to be honest. 'Tis but a filthy piece of work.

Painter You're a dog.

Column 2 *(to Column 1)* Ape.

Ape   Thy *mother's* of my generation; what's *she* if I be a dog?

(painter is visibly offended)

Poet   The dog and the ape were bent out of shape.

Ape   Shut up, Poet.

Timon   Wilt thou dine with us, Apemantus? Most welcome are ye to my fortunes—prithee, let my meat make thee silent.

Ape   I scorn thy meat; 'twould choke me, for I should ne'er flatter thee. O you gods, what a number of men eats Timon, and he sees 'em not! It grieves me to see so many dip their meat in one man's blood. I wonder men dare trust themselves with men. There's much example for it; the fellow that sits next to him, now parts bread with him, is the readiest man to kill him; it has been proved.

Timon   Nonsense, Apemantus. These be my friends. *(patting Poet on the back)* What need have we of any friends, if we should ne'er have need of 'em? 'Twould resemble sweet instruments hung up in cases, that keep their sounds to themselves. Were it the *other* way 'round, and were *I* the poorer, they would provide for *me*, to be sure.

Painter We're out of ale!

Jeweler We're out of meat!

Poet We're out of pudding!

Timon Then I will purchase some more.

Column 1 Um, no you won't. You're out of gold.

Timon What?

Column 2 Kaput, vanished, squandered, vaporized—you gave it all away!

Timon Who will help me?

Jeweler Not I, *(exits with bags of gold)*

Column 1 said the Jeweler.

Painter Not I, *(exits with bags of gold)*

Column 2 said the Painter.

Poet Not I, *(exits with bags of gold)*

Column 1 said the Poet.

Ventidius Not I, *(exits with bags of gold)*

Column 2 said Ventidius, wrapped in prison sheets.

Lucilius Not I, *(running through with his maid, dressed in finery)*

Column 1 said Lucilius, with his girlfriend.

Queen Not I,

Column 2 said Good Queen Bess, stuffing her jewels into her dress.

Ape Told ya so!

Column 1 said the Ape man.

Ape Here, I will mend thy feast. *(hands him a root)*

Timon First mend my company; take away thy*self*.

Ape Thou shouldst have hated thy mockers sooner and loved thyself better.

Timon What wouldst *thou* do with the world, Apemantus, if it lay in *thy* power?

Ape Give it to the beasts, to be rid of the men.

Timon A beastly ambition. If thou wert the lion, the fox would beguile thee; if thou wert the lamb, the fox would eat thee; if thou wert the fox, the lion would suspect thee when peradventure thou wert accused by the ass; if thou wert the ass, thy dullness would torment thee, and still thou livedst as breakfast to the wolf; if thou wert the wolf, thy greediness would afflict thee; wert thou the unicorn, pride and wrath would confound thee and make thine own self the conquest of thy fury. . . What beast couldst thou be that were not subject to a beast?

Ape Athens is become a forest of beasts, and thou art the cap of all the fools alive.

Timon Away, thou tedious rogue! I am sorry I shall lose a stone by thee! *(throws the rock at Apemantus, and he leaves)*
I am sick of this false world. Timon, presently prepare thy grave. *(He starts "digging" his own grave—N1 and N3 go help him—then he jumps in.)* And so die. I am quit. *(He dies, and N1 and N3 "bury" him.)*

(Narrators, queen, and columns stare at him for a bit, then look at each other.)

Queen *(clapping)* Bravo! Am I the unicorn? My people usually call me the pelican.

N2 That was depressing.

Column 1 Moral:

Column 2 Better a borrower than a lender be.

Column 1 Bolonius.

N1 Well, I think we've seen enough of the Greeks.

(Timon gets up, takes a bow and exits—Columns exit.)

N2 On to the Romans?

N1 *(Googling)* Ooh—listen to this cast list: Coriolanus, Cominius, Menenius, Volumnia, Valeria. They *all* sound like body parts or diseases.

N3 This one is about an arrogant Roman general named Caius Marcius who loathes the common people.

(Coriolanus enters arrogantly with fanfare music—Volumnia and Valeria follow.)

N3 Spurred on by his controlling ambitious mother. . .

Queen Can I be the mother? I have always wanted to be a *real* mother and not just a *symbolic* mother to my people.

(N1, N2, and N3 all put their hands over their necks and look at each other with concern—N3 motions to the actor dressed as the mother to hand over her costume.)

N2 Of course, your majesty. You may be Volumnia.

N3 You're sort of overdressed. You'll need to wear this. *(pointing to mother's costume)*

Queen Uh, never mind then—that gown will never do. I'll just watch.

(Volumnia resumes position with the Romans; Queen settles back on her throne.)

Coriolanus *(steps forward and yells at audience)* I have nothing but contempt for you plebeians P-L-E-B-E-I-A-N-S! *(pronounced: pliˈbēəns with accent on second syllable)*

N3 *(to narrators)* Oh, oops. I guess the audience is playing the part of the plebeians.

N1 And the army.

N2 So, we are going to divide you in half, right down the middle.

(motions an imaginary line down the audience—N1 and N3 each take a side—N2 goes from side to side to help with upcoming repeats)

N3 *(to audience)* You pathetic people on *this* side will be the plebeians, with me. We are hungry and fed up with Coriolanus. Be angry. You will repeat after me when I raise my arm. *(raising arm to practice)* Like this! [Like this!]

N1 And those of us on *this* side will be Coriolanus's army. We're the bad guys, full of tyranny! Repeat after me when I raise my arm. *(raises it)* Got it? [Got it!]

N2 *(to narrators)* I think they can handle it. They look hungry and warrior-like. Alright, Coriolanus, start again.

Coriolanus *(steps forward and yells at audience)* I have nothing but contempt for you plebeians P-L-E-B-E-I-A-N-S!

N1 *(raising arm)* We want our grain! [We want our grain!]

Coriolanus Too bad! You plebeians are not worthy of grain. Now I'm going off to war, so say no more! *(to Volumnia, cheerfully)* How am I doing, Mother?

Volumnia Good job, Caius Marcius. I am so proud of you. Now go take over another city.

Coriolanus *(skips to another city)* Here I am, with my army, to devastate the city of Corioli C-O-R-I-O-L-I!

N1 *(raising arm)* Open the gates! [Open the gates!]

N3 *(raising arm)* Don't let him in! [Don't let him in!]

(He storms the city—or rather, the audience storms each other! Coriolanus goes backstage to quickly get bloodied.)

N1 *(raising arm)* Chaaarge! [Chaaarge!]

N3 *(raising arm)* Aaaaahhh! [Aaaaahhh!]

N1 *(raising arm)* Take that! [Take that!]

N3 *(raising arm)* Help us! [Help us!]

N1 *(raising arm)* Die, Coriolis! [Die Coriolis!]

(N1 attacks N3's leg, and he falls to the ground.)

N3 *(raising arm while lying on the ground)* Oww! [Oww!] My leg! [My leg!] We don't want to die! [We don't want to die!] We just want our grain! [We just want our grain!] We like pancakes! [We like pancakes!] *(N1 stabs N3 to shut him up.)* Oh crap! [Oh crap!]

(N2 goes to N3 and pushes his arm down.)

N2 I think you've been conquered.

N1 *(raising arm)* Yeah! [Yeah!]

(Coriolanus re-enters, all bloodied and wounded.)

Coriolanus Mother, I'm home! We did it! Corioli belongs to the Romans now! *(sitting and whining)* I have some wounds upon me, and they hurt O-U-C-H!

Volumnia Well done, son!

Valeria You rock, butcher block!

Coriolanus Poppycock! 'Twas a cake walk. *(to Valeria)* Who are you?

Valeria Valeria. Rhymes with malaria. I do your laundry. You have some stains. Can I have your clothes? *(pulls on them)* Well, after we finish this scene.

Coriolanus *(to the ladies)* Mother, malaria girl, they gave me a new name after the town I defeated. I am now Coriolanus *(stands up)* C-O-R-I-O-L-A-N-U-S!

N3 *(sitting up)* Why, because he sat on it? *(jumping up with excitement)* Ooh ooh, then can I be Meneniusrectus? *(emphasize the rectus)*

N1 Can I be Cominiusorifice? *(likewise!)*

Coriolanus Oh look—here comes Gluteus Maximus! *(Captain Undergarments enters.)*

Captain U Coriolanus, the plebeians want their grain.

Coriolanus But Mother says. . .

N3 Coriolanus, the plebeians are tired of you breaking their legs and burning their homes.

Coriolanus But, Meneniusrectus, Mother says. . .

N1 Coriolanus, the people want you to leave.

Coriolanus But, Cominiusorifice, Mother says. . .

N3 *(raising his arm)* Send him away! [Send him away!]

Coriolanus *(pops into a childish British accent)* Mother, how come the plebeians don't like me? Do you think it's my new name? They want to send me away.

Volumnia My dear son, I have affectionately and shrewdly raised you to be a brutal warrior. When you were but tender-bodied, I was pleased to let you seek danger where you were like to find fame. To a cruel war I sent you, and your bloodied brow proved yourself a man. Had I a dozen sons, each in my love alike, I had rather eleven die nobly for their country than one voluptuously surfeit out of action.

But maybe I was all wrong. You don't seem to have any friends. Let's try a different tactic. How about you try being nice to people and bring peace and give them their grain.

Coriolanus Aww. Let me have war; it exceeds peace as far as day does night; it's spritely, waking, audible, and full of vent. Peace is a very apoplexy, lethargy: mulled, deaf, sleepy, insensible. B-O-R-I-N-G.

Volumnia Anie. . .

Coriolanus Okay, Mother. Whatever you say. *(addressing the audience)* Peace, plebeians. You may have peace!

N3   *(raising arm)* We don't want peas! [We don't want peas!] We want our grain! [We want our grain!] Tear him to pieces! [Tear him to pieces!]

(N1 and Captain Undergarments haul Coriolanus away as he yells to his mother—Valeria follows.)

Coriolanus Mother, they are taking me away! They are going to tear me to pieces.

Volumnia Um, don't I have any more lines?

N3   Nope.

Volumnia They just assassinate my son, and I don't get to say anything about it?

N3   That's right; but nice pun!

N2   This play sure was heinous

N3   Yep, that's Coriolanus.

(Volumnia bows and exits—N1 stays backstage to prepare for Macbuff.)

N2   Boy, the Romans weren't any better than the Greeks. I think it's time for some comedy. I'm ready for a twin romance play.

N3   Why stop with twins? How about cross-dressing twins, to add to the confusion? Set in ancient Illyria on the eastern coast of the Adriatic, *Twelfth Night*, or *What You Will*, involves a pair of twins who are mistaken for each other.

Queen The twelfth night after Christmas is a time of great revelry in my land! Hush, here come the lovers!

(enter Duke Orsino and a musician, Valentine—musician makes some music on a recorder or something, the less skill the better)

Orsino *(lovesick)*

If music be the food of love, play on;
give me excess of it, that surfeiting
the appetite may sicken and so die. *(pause for music)*
That strain again! It had a dying fall.
O, it came o'er my ear like the sweet sound
that breathes upon a bank of violets,
stealing and giving odor. *(sniffs a shoe—more bad music)* Enough, no more.
'Tis not so sweet now as it was before. *(music stops)*
O, when mine eyes did see Olivia first,
that instant was I turned into a hart;
and my desires, like fell and cruel hounds,
e'er since pursue me.

Queen Excuse me, with *whom* is the Duke in love?

Valentine The lady Olivia, who doesn't care that he exists.

N2 Oh look! Here come the twins. They don't look so good.

N3 That's because they've been shipwracked.

(Sebastian is seen to the side struggling with a wave, swimming, etc. Viola swims to shore, panting—or she could arrive by inflatable whale, swim noodle, motorboat. . .)

Viola *(to narrators)* What country, friends, is this?

N3 This is Illyria, lady.

Viola And what should I do in Illyria?

Valentine Well, I suggest you dress up like a guy and go serve that lovesick Duke. But I'll warn you, he is going to make you woo Olivia for him, you are probably going to fall in love with him, and Olivia is likely to fall in love with you, thinking you are a guy, of course.

Viola O-kay. Here, take my skirt. *(pulls off skirt and tucks her hair into a hat so that she now is dressed identical to Sebastian)* But what about my poor twin brother? Perchance he is not drowned?

(Sebastian is still off to the side, struggling in the water.)

Valentine Perchance. I saw your brother, most provident in peril, bind himself to a strong mast that liv'd upon the sea:

To Do or NOT to Do...

where, like Arion on the dolphin's back, I saw him hold acquaintance with the waves so long as I could see.

Viola Hold acquaintance with the waves? That's a good sign, right? Well, I have nothing better to do in this foreign land, so I will go see this Duke Orsino. Is he good-looking? Do you think he'll think I'm pretty?

N3 You're a guy, remember?

Viola *(deepening voice and adjusting pants)* Oh, right. Call me *Cesario*.

Valentine Come, *Cesario*. Time to meet the Duke.

(They cross the stage to where the Duke is obsessing over a shoe worn by Olivia.)

Valentine Ahem, Sir Duke. This young man, or boy rather, just washed up on our shores and would like to serve you. His name is *Cesario*.

Orsino Just in time, too! Have *I* a job for you! A *lady* we must woo! Here, sniff her shoe! *(sniffs the shoe and holds it out for Viola to smell)*

Viola Ew.

Orsino *(to Valentine)* Who are you?

Valentine Uh, Valentine.

Orsino A Valentine! Great idea! You will be a Valentine sent to my lady, Olivia! *(dresses Viola ridiculously as a giant heart)*

Viola *(manly)* I'll do my best to woo your lady. *(aside)* Though I must confess, I think he's rather cute and romantic. Except for the shoe-sniffing thing.

Valentine And good luck getting past Malvolio.

Viola Who's that?

Valentine My evil twin.

(Viola ventures across stage to where Olivia has appeared, looking a lot like Orsino. Valentine runs across and jumps in front of Olivia, puts on an evil twin mustache and goatee, and acts as Malvolio.)

Viola So, you must be Malvolio. I'd like to see Olivia.

Malvolio *(evilly)* Would you? *(to Olivia)* Madam, yond young youth yearns to yack with you.

Olivia *(perhaps a random Southern accent)* What kind o' man is he?

Malvolio Uhhh. . .*(looking at Viola)* kind of girly. Not yet old enough for a man nor young enough for a boy: as a squash is before 'tis a pescod, or a codling when 'tis almost a codpiece. He is very well favor'd, and he speaks very shrewishly.

Olivia Let him approach.

Viola Most radiant, exquisite, and unmatchable beauty. 'Tis beauty truly blent, whose red and white visage nature's own sweet and cunning hand hath laid on. Lady, you are the cruelest she alive if you will lead these graces to the grave and leave the world no copy.

Olivia Go on. Pri*thee*, more praise of my beauty. *(flaunting herself)*

Viola I can say no more than I have studied. I speak for my master, not for myself.

Olivia But you haven't finished taking inventory of my attributes. What about my two blushing cheeks; my two blue eyes with lids on them *(batting them)*; my one smooth neck; my one dimpled chin *(jutting it out)*; my two shiny red lips *(sticking them out)*; my translucent, blemish-free, wrinkle-free skin *(grabs Viola's hand and makes her feel her face)*; my ten, glossy, recently buffed and manicured fingernails *(extending them toward Viola, who backs away)*; my delicate, elegant, artistic arms *(lifts them over her head)*; my two, pirouetting, size six and a half feet *(dancing with some ballet leaps, twirls and poses)*; my duet of flawlessly formed knees *(lifting skirt to reveal knees)*; my. . . ? *(still lifting skirt)*

N2 *(cutting her off)* Ahem!

Olivia *(dropping skirt)* Weren't you sent hither to praise me?

Viola Oh yes, my master suffers with adorations, fertile tears, with groans that thunder love, with sighs of fire. . .

Olivia Your lord does not know my mind: I cannot love him. But *you*. . .

Viola Umm, I gotta go. *(runs off, but accidently loses a shoe)*

Olivia Malvolio, run after that peevish boy. Bring him back to me!

(Olivia picks up the shoe and sniffs it. Viola runs toward Orsino, but stops mid-stage to shake off the heebie jeebies. Malvolio runs back to Orsino and becomes Valentine.)

Viola *(throwing off giant heart garb)* Is that *really* how Shakespeare wrote this?

N3 Well, no. We're taking it easy on you.

Viola Can we just skip to the part where we fall in love with guys?

Olivia *(holding up shoe)* Does this shoe fit anyone else?

(Sebastian, who has been swimming around, finally makes it to shore, on Olivia's side of the stage. He is covered with fish and assorted sea things. But nobody notices him yet, except the audience.)

Sebastian *(dragging himself to shore, sits facing audience, feeling the "land" beneath him)* Oh, look! Land! *(then busies himself dumping sand out of his shoes, banging water out of his ears, pulling off crustaceans, etc.)*

(attention shifts to Orsino's side of Illyria)

Orsino Look, here comes our Valentine.

Valentine No, *I'm* Valentine.

N2 I thought he was Malvolio

Orsino *(to Viola)* Does she *love* me, Cesario?

Viola She does *love*, sir.

Orsino But does she love *me*, sir?

Viola She loves your *words*, sir.

Orsino But loves she the *man* behind the words, sir?

Viola *That* she does, sir.

Orsino So, she *loves* me!

Viola Were *I* her, *I* would love thee.

Orsino You speak in riddles, just like a woman, Cesario.

Viola I can't help it, sir. *(taking off her other shoe and coquettishly dropping it in front of Orsino)*

Valentine What happened to your other shoe?

Viola *(horrified)* Oh no!

(action shifts to Olivia side of stage)

Sebastian *(to narrators)* What country, friends, is this?

N3 This is Illyria, dude.

Sebastian And what should I do in Illyria?

(Valentine switches back into Malvolio.)

Malvolio Well, I suggest you go visit that lady over there. Her name is Olivia.

Sebastian *(loudly)* Olivia?

Olivia You have returned. Will you marry me?

Sebastian *(to the audience)* So, this is how they do things in Illyria? *(to Olivia)* Well, you do have two eyes with lids on them. Sure, I'll marry you.

Olivia To the church, then! Come, Cesario! Here, put your shoe back on! *(hands him Viola's shoe)*

Sebastian My shoe? Cesario?

(action switches back to Orsino's side)

Orsino She loves me! To the church, then! Come, Cesario! Put your shoe back on!

(Orsino and Viola lock eyes awkwardly for a moment as he reluctantly hands her the shoe. Valentine/Malvolio can't decide who to be and ends up putting the mustache and goatee on one side of his face. Sebastian sniffs Viola's shoe and says, "Viola?" All head to center of stage for the surprise reunion.)

Sebastian *(seeing Viola)* My sis. . .brother?

Viola *(seeing her shoe first and then her brother)* My shoe! My brother!

(They embrace.)

Sebastian Then you are not drowned; but art thou my sister?

Viola My father had a mole upon his brow.

To Do or NOT to Do...

Sebastian   And so had mine!   Sister, Viola, mend thyself! *(attempts to cover her lower half)*

Orsino   How have you made division of yourself? An apple cleft in two is not more twin than these two creatures.

Queen   Identical twins!

N3   Well, not exactly.

Olivia   Which one of you is Cesario, the man I am to marry?

Sebastian   So it seems, lady, you have been mistook. You are engaged both to a maid and a man.

Olivia   Well, which one of you is the man? If *he* is you, then who are you?

Viola   *(releasing hair from hat)*   A girl sir, or lady rather. This is so confusing. I don't know what I am anymore!

Olivia   Eenie, meenie, minee, mo. . .*(and then pointing to Sebastian, or not!)*

N2   Isn't that a Justin Bieber song?

Olivia   I'll take that one. You look just like her, but you're a guy, right? Then I will marry you, Cesario.

Sebastian   Sebastian.

Orsino   *(to Viola)*   Now you're a woman named Viola? If this be so, then I shall have a share in this most happy wrack! I love you! Give me thy *(Viola holds out her hand)* shoe *(then hands him her shoe with a delighted smile)*, and let me see thee in thy woman's weeds!

Olivia   *(to Orsino)*   It never would have worked out between us, you know. We're too much alike.

(Valentine brings Sebastian the skirt, who puts it on as if out of habit, and then the two couples stand arm-in-arm on either side of Valentine/Malvolio.)

Queen   They're like a mirror image of each other!

N3   Well, not exactly.

O&O   *(turning toward Valentine/Malvolio, together)*   Who are you?

Valentine   Malvalentine? I'm a bifacial twin! *(showing audience both sides of his face)*   Moral: Some are born girl, some achieve manhood, some have cross-dressing thrust apon 'em.

(Valentine plays some music while the two couples exit.)

Queen   Enough of your music. Be gone.

N2   Oh my. Shakespeare sure was. . .twi-sted.

N3   Three down, six to go? One more before intermission? We're gonna be cuttin' it close.

N2   How about something less romantic? That one gave me indigestion.

N3   A quick one then, like the Scottish play. We'll consolidate.

(N1 returns with two actors who will be playing Banquo and Lady Macbeth)

Banquo Gonna have to, cause we're all you've got. Everyone else is back there eating haggis.

Lady Mac Well, they're calling it haggis, but really it's just pudding.

N2   What is haggis, exactly? *(to N1)* Google it.

N1   *(googling)* "Haggis is a kind of savoury pudding containing sheep's 'pluck' (heart, liver and lungs), minced with onion, oatmeal, suet, spices, and salt, mixed with stock, and traditionally encased in the animal's stomach and simmered for approximately three hours."

N3   Mmmm!

N2   Excuse me. *(holding hands over mouth and running off stage)*

N1   So, just the four of us for the Scottish play?

N3   What about the weird sisters? They're caught up in haggis, too?

Banquo They say they're being type-cast.

N3   Of course they're being type-cast.

Lady Mac This is all *your* fault. You fix it. *(leaves)*

N3   Fine, I'll be the weird sisters.

Banquo All three of them?

N3   Sure. *(becoming witchy and Scottish)* Double Double toil and trrrrrrouble. . . *(cackles and goes off to become three witches—dresses himself in witch get-up and prepares two hand puppets or dolls: a girly pig puppet and a bearded rat or rodent)*

Queen   *(becoming interested)*   My nephew, James IV of Scotland, is really into this witch stuff.

Banquo   Uh—perhaps Good Queen Bess can be useful! Would you like to. . .?

Queen   *(cutting him off)*   Nay! I would never help the Scots. We don't really get along. But you may do your play. As long as they all DIE!

(While waiting for N3 to return, N1 and Banquo play bagpipe music and march around to set a "Scottish" mood. N3 returns with a cauldron, portraying three witches—Weird Sister 3 is the girly pig puppet. N3, as himself, is Weird Sister 1. WS1 and WS3 watch as Weird Sister 2 (the rat puppet) arrives from behind N3's back. Sure hope that makes sense—a clever actor can pull this off! N3 uses three different voices for the witches. For a "Scottish" feel, actors could have fun rolling their rrrrr's.)

N3/WS1   Where hast thou been, sister?

N3/WS2   *(rat voice)* Killing swine.

N3/WS3   *(outraged Miss Piggy voice)*   What! What do you mean, killing swine?! Why you little. . .Hi-yah!

(A fight ensues between the puppet witches as they yell at each other.)

N3/WS2   A sailor's wife had chestnuts in her lap, and munched, and munched, and munched like a pig: "Give me," quoth I. And she wouldn't share, so I. . .

N3/WS3   You're like a rat without a tail. I'll give thee a wind.

N3/WS2   Show me! Show me! *(more fighting)*

(a drum is heard)

N3/WS1   A drum! A drum! Macbeth doth come!

(fighting stops, and they all watch—Macbeth and Banquo approach)

Macbeth   So foul and fair a day I have not seen.

N3/WS2 Fair is foul,

N3/WS3 and foul is fair.

Banquo What are these, so withered and so wild in their attire, that look not like the inhabitants o' the earth? You should be women, and yet your beards forbid me to interpret that you are so, and one of you looks like a pig.

N3/WS3 Oui! C'est moi!

Macbeth Speak, if you can: what are you?

N3/WS3 Scottish swine, to you, buster.

N3/WS1 All hail, Macbeth! thane of Glamis!

N3/WS2 All hail, Macbeth, thane of Cawdor!

N3/WS3 All hail, Macbeth, thou shalt be king hereafter!

Banquo What about me?

N3/WS1 Uh. . . Hail Banquo! Lesser than Macbeth and greater!

N3/WS2 Not so happy, yet much happier!

N3/WS3 Thou shalt get kings, though thou be none—whatever that means!

All three Macbeth and Banquo, all hail!

(N3 tosses witch puppets into the cauldron and leaves—they are heard yelling, "let us out, sister! We don't want to be cooked with the entrails!")

Banquo The earth hath bubbles, and these are of them. Whither are they vanished?

Macbeth Your children shall be kings!

Banquo You shall be king!

Macbeth Well, since father conveniently died, I'm already the thane of Glamis. But the thane of Cawdor lives. Look, here comes my lovely wife, Lady Mac.

Banquo *(aside)* 'N Cheese.

(Lady Macbeth enters.)

Lady Mac *(excited and perhaps a bit crazy)* Guess what, husband? King Duncan had the thane of Cawdor executed and now we, I mean you, are the thane of Cawdor!

To Do or NOT to Do...

Queen *(to Lady Mac)* This is sort of like how I became queen. First, father died, and of course my disgusting little half-brother Edward got to become king at the age of nine just because he was a boy. Then that little idiot died at the age of 15 and some random cousin named Jane Grey pretended to be queen for nine days until my bloody half-sister Mary had her deposed. I thought Mary was my friend until she locked me in that tower. And a few years later, she died—I think something was wrong with her, you know, girl parts. How many more people need to die before *you* become king?

Lady Mac Well, let's see... there's King Duncan.

Queen Just one? That will never do.

(Two actors walk through eating pudding. Lady Macbeth and the Queen strangle them, then eat their pudding.)

Lady Mac Mmmm, I love tapioca haggis.

Queen Yes, that's more like it! You definitely have the stomach for it.

(Macbeth and Banquo drag the bodies off stage.)

Macbeth *(returning and pondering over himself as a king)* Come what come may, time and the hour runs through the roughest day.

Lady Mac What are you talking about? We have a murder to plan.

Macbeth Huh?

Lady Mac King Duncan, you dunce! I do fear thy nature is too full of the milk of human kindness. *(handing donut-shaped crown to Banquo)* Here, you be King Duncan.

Ban/Duncan Okay. *(looking at crown)* This looks like a donut. *(putting on crown)*

Lady Mac *(to Duncan)* Would you like to have a slumber party at our house tonight?

Macbeth Great idea, wife! Honey, can we stay up all night playing bagpipes and eating chocolate haggis skins?

Ban/Duncan Sounds like pure Scottish fun. I'm in.

Lady Mac Well, here's your bed chamber, and here's your haggis. Go to bed now.

Macbeth Aww. Do we have to? We didn't get to play bagpipes yet.

Lady Mac Not you—get over here. *(Macbeth marches obediently to his wife.)* Did you even *read* this play? You have to kill King Duncan while he is sleeping.

Macbeth But that will ruin our slumber party!

Lady Mac That's the idea.

Queen He ate all your chocolate haggis skins.

Macbeth Then he *dies!* If it were done when 'tis done, then 'twere well it were done quickly! Away, and mock the time with fairest show. False face must hide what the false heart doth know. *(to Lady Mac)* See, I studied it.

Lady Mac That's more like it. Screw your courage to the sticking place, and we'll not fail. Here is a dagger. *(hands it to him)* It belongs to someone else, so it won't look like you did it.

Macbeth *(getting all dramatic, downstage center)*
    Is this a dagger which I see before me?
    The handle toward my hand? Come, let me clutch thee.
    I have thee not, and yet I see thee still.
    Art thou not, fatal vision, sensible to feeling
    as to sight? *(pokes it)* Ouch.
    Or art thou but a dagger of the mind, a false creation,
    proceeding from the heat-oppressèd brain?
    I see thee yet, in form as palpable
    as this which now I draw.
(draws with it in the air)
    Mine eyes are made the fools of the other senses.
    I see thee still, and on thy blade and dudgeon
    gouts of blood, which was not so before.

Lady Mac Would you just get on with it? You were supposed to do the stabbing somewhere in the middle of your monologue.

Macbeth Where? Should I start over?

Lady Mac No, just go do it, and I'll say my lines.

(Macbeth goes and stabs Duncan, who already appears to be dead, then goes backstage.)

Lady Mac That which hath made them drunk

To Do or NOT to Do...

hath made me bold.
What hath quenched them hath given me fire.
Hark!
(a very long, horrifying scream is heard from backstage)
It was the owl that shrieked, the fatal bellman,
which gives the stern'st good-night.
He is about it. My husband?

(Macbeth returns with three bloody daggers.)
Macbeth I have done the deed. He didn't even flinch.

Lady Mac That's because I poisoned the pudding, just in case.

Macbeth They must have *all* eaten your pudding, cause those other guys didn't even flinch either.

Lady Mac What other guys? *(looking backstage)* You murdered the set crew?

Macbeth Actually, I think *you* murdered them with your evil haggis. And since they were already dead, my conscience is clear. Here, take the bloody daggers. Who's next?

Queen You two rock!

Banquo *(getting up and taking off donut crown)* Can I go back to being Banquo, now that Duncan's dead?

Macbeth If your children shall be kings, then *(stabs him)* take this. *(Banquo falls)* Rats. I forget to ask him where his children are hiding. Who's next?

Lady Mac *(smearing blood on herself from the daggers)* My hands are of your color, but I shame to wear a heart so white. Go get some water and wash this filthy witness from your hands. Why did you bring these daggers from the place? The sleeping and the dead are but as pictures. 'Tis the eye of childhood that fears a painted devil. I hear a knocking at the south entry. *(Banquo jumps up, runs across stage and makes a knocking sound.)* Someone's here. *(Banquo makes more knocking.)* Thou canst not wake *them* with thy knocking. A little water clears us of this deed.

Banquo *(returning, nonchalantly)* What's wrong with her?

Macbeth She got some blood on her hands. Now who are you?

(Queen tosses Banquo a scarf and some doll babies.)

Banquo *(womanly)* Macduff's wife and children.

Macbeth *(pulls out Shakespeare book and scans it)* Yep, you're on my list. *(stabs them)*

Lady Mac Children?

Macbeth We have scorched the snake, not killed it!

(Banquo ditches the children and arises again, this time with a white sheet over him—best to plant the sheet on stage before scene!)

Ban/ghost Oooooh, aaaahhhhh!

Macbeth Back for more? Who are ya this time?

Ban/ghost Banquo's ghoooooost. You can't kill a ghooooost! I'm already dead!

Macbeth Avaunt, and quit my sight! Let the earth hide thee.

Ban/ghost My bones are maaaarrowless; my blood is cooooold. *(reaching out)*

Lady Mac Blood! Blood! I murdered them! They're coming back to haunt me.

Macbeth *(aside)* It was all her idea, and *she's* the one who can't handle it. Blood will have blood, they say. *(to ghost)* Since you're out haunting and being all creepy, will you fetch me those weird sisters?

Ban/ghost By the strength of my illooosion, I'll draw them here for your confuoooosion.

Macbeth *(seeing Lady)* Great, now she's sleepwalking.

Lady Mac *(rubbing her hands)* Hell is murky. Who would have thought the old man to have so much blood in him? What, will these hands ne'er be clean? Yet here's a spot.

(Banquo actor returns playfully on all fours as Spot, with dog ears and nose and tongue out, panting. Lady Macbeth sees the dog and yells at him!)

Lady Mac Out, damned spot, out, I say!

Ban/dog Ruff.

Lady Mac *(confused)* Out, damned Ruff, out, I say!

(dog whimpers and goes to Macbeth, who pets him while N3 returns as weird sisters and sets up cauldron)

Lady Mac *(wandering and sniffing her hand)* Here's the smell of blood still. All the perfumes of Arabia will not sweeten this little hand. *(She wanders off.)*

N3/WS1 Round about the cauldron go; in the poisoned entrails throw. Eye of newt and toe of frog, wool of bat and tongue of dog. *(cackles and looks at dog, who flees the stage)*

N3/WS2 Fillet of a stupid pig, snorting in her greasy wig.

(W3 puppet gets angry at W2 puppet and retaliates.)

N3/WS3 Liver of a scurvy rat—cut it out, or you'll go splat!

N3/WS2 Slice of bacon, slab of pork; ham and hotdogs skewered with fork!

(The two puppets fight.)

N3/WS1 Ladies, hush! By the pricking of my thumbs, something wicked this way comes!

WS1/WS2/WS3 Macbeth! Macbeth! Macbeth!

Macbeth *(approaching)* Had I three ears, I'd hear thee. What else can you hags tell me?

N3/WS2 Beware Macduff!

N3/WS3 Be bloody, bold, and resolute, for none of woman born shall harm Macbeth.

N3/WS1 Macbeth shall never vanquished be until Great Birnam Wood come against him.

Macbeth Right, like the trees can uproot and come get me. What do you mean, "none of woman born"? Like that's possible! I can handle Macduff. Bring it on!

WS1/WS2/WS3 We warned you, buckaroo! *(They cackle, dance and exit.)*

(Banquo returns as Birnam Wood with branches and attacks Macbeth.)

Macbeth *(sarcastically)* Ooh, scary—trees! Oak or maple, spruce or pine? I'll hack you into kindling, one at a time. *(chops at tree actor who gives up after losing branches and falls down)* Alright, you can get up now so I can kill Macduff.

Ban/trees *(getting up and gathering broken branches, angry and exhausted)* No, this part stinks! I'm done dying! I'm going on intermission! Good luck killing Macduff all by yourself! *(leaves)*

Macbeth *(looks around and realizes he is the only one left on stage, except for the Queen, who has fallen asleep)* So, it looks like it's just me and me, and I still have to kill Macduff. Macbeth *and* Macduff at the same time. . . I guess that makes me Macbuff! Yeah, Macbuff! *(flexing muscles)* And I kinda need to use the men's room, so I better make this quick. *(stabs at himself, but he doesn't die)* Why won't I die? *(switches places with himself)* Turn, hellhound, turn! *(switches)* I'll fight till from my bones my flesh be hacked. *(switches)* Fight all you want. You can't kill me. I was not of woman born. *(switches—confused)* But then how. . . ? Eww! *(switches and stabs, then switches and falls)*

(N3 and Banquo return and stand over Macbuff's body.)

Banquo Finally.

N3 Let's let the audience take a break while we mop up all this blood.

(Scottish bagpipe music is played. They drag Macbuff backstage.

To Do or NOT to Do. . .

INTERMISSION

(Queen Elizabeth is still sleeping. She can sleep through intermission on stage or leave and go back to sleep on stage before second half begins. Music transitions into Renaissance style or something spritely.)

ACT 2

(Queen is asleep on stage. Lymetrius plants himself in front row of audience and sleeps. Annie/Puck enters, mopping the floor. She continues to clean a spot on the side as N1 and N3 enter.)

N1 Shhh! The queen is sleeping. That's a relief!

N3 *(to N1)* That was quite a bloody mess you made of that Scottish play. What ever happened to Lady Macbeth?

N1 I'm not sure what happened to Lady Macbeth. *(sees N2 entering and flexes arms to show off)* But I sure was buff.

N3 *(to N2)* Hey, pudding breath! Feeling any better?

N2 I am, no thanks to you two. Lady Macbeth is in the ladies' room. Act One was rather dark. How about we lighten things up?

N3 Dost thou like fairies?

N2 *(excited)* Oh yes! 'Tis fairy time!

(N3 goes and trades Puck's mop for broom.)

N3 Well, what are *you* waiting for? Go get your wings!

Puck *(singing to the tune of "It's a Hard Knock Life")* I'll put a girdle round the stage in just fourteen seconds flat; I'll get my wings and I'll be back, da da da da da. . . *(goes backstage)*

N1 *A Midsummer Night's Dream.* Isn't that the confusing one with the plot within a plot within a plot?

N2 Yeah.

N3 Why don't we just focus on the chick fights and donkey love?

(Captain Undergarments enters on one side, eating an apple.)

N1 I think we have our ass. *(pointing at CU)*

N2 And we will need one tall blonde and one short brunette. Do we really need two men? I can't tell them apart anyway.

N3 So let's just conserve actors and call him Lymetrius . . . or Demander.

N1 I'll go personally select the two girls for the chick fight.

N3 *(deviously)* And I will go seek Oberon, king of the fairies! *(laughing evilly)*

N2 That leaves me to hold down the stage, I guess. *(looking at sleeping queen and then going over to set a pillow under her head, and perhaps surrounding her with comfortable things, like stuffed fairies)* If we are lucky, she will *never* wake up. She smells like she is 400 years old—I don't think they had deodorant back then. In fact, I read somewhere that they used something called a pomander, which was a kind of ball filled with herbs to disguise nasty smells. *(sees the queen's small pomander and holds it up)* Oh look! She actually has one. This is not *nearly* big enough. I'll go see what I can do.

(N1 enters with a tall brunette and a short blonde, or two tall blondes—or whatever they happen to be—Helena and Hermia.)

N1 I found some pretty girls.

Helena *(to N1)* Call you *me* fair? that fair again unsay.
        Lymetrius loves *her (pointing to Hermia)* fair:
        O happy fair!
        Her eyes are lode-stars; and *her* tongue's sweet air.
        Sickness is catching: Achoo!
(smearing snot on sleeve)
        O, were favour so; *(to Hermia, dramatically)*
        Yours would *I* catch, fair Hermia, ere I go;
        My ear should catch *your* voice, my eye *your* eye,
        My tongue should catch *your* tongue's sweet melody.
        Were the world mine, Lymetrius being bated,
        The rest I'd give to be to *you* translated.
        O, teach me how you look, and with what art
        You sway the motion of Lymetrius' heart.

Hermia I don't even know the guy. You can have him. I'm in love with *Demander*. But of course my father hates him, so we are going to run away together into the dark and scary woods. It will be so romantic: vines and tree bark, campfires, marshmallows, slimy snakes and quick sand from which he can rescue me, F.O.U.S's...

N3 *(returning)* I don't believe they exist.

Helena What are F.O.U.S.'s?

(Captain Undergarments wanders in on the side)
Captain U *(fanning the air near his backside)* Flatulence of unbelievable stench!

(Hermia glares at him, and he leaves.)
Hermia No, Fairies Of Unusual Size! *(shaking with excitement)* Gives me goosebumps just thinking about it.

Helena You're nuts. Come on; I'll help you pack. *(They leave, with Helena giving her a list of supplies as they walk off.)* You're gonna need a frame pack, inflatable air mattress, hiking boots, an extra petticoat. . .

Puck *(entering and singing, Annie style)*
How now, spirits, whither wander you?
Over hill, over dale, thorough bush, thorough brier?
Over park, over pale, thorough flood, thorough fire?

N1 Aren't you supposed to be Puck?

Puck *(to N1)* Thou speakest aright; I am that merry wanderer of the night. I jest to Oberon and make him smile when *I* a fat and bean-fed horse beguile. *(stops, not knowing what kind of action to use)* Umm, what's beguile?

N1 *(Googling)* Uh. . .

Puck Yay—here comes Oberon!

Oberon *(entering, with green face paint and wings)* Welcome, wanderer. Hast thou the flower there?

Puck What flower? *(reaching into pocket and pulling it out)* Silly me—I mean, aye, there it is! *(waving it around)*

Oberon I pray thee *give* it me. *(grabs it)* I'm ticked off at Titania, and I feel like playing a nasty trick on her. Where is my queen? *(looking around)*

(N2 and N3 roll in a giant "pomander" covered with herbs and put it beside the sleeping queen)

Oberon *(agitated)* I repeat, where is my queen?

N1 *(to N2 and N3)* We need a queen!

N3 *(pointing to sleeping Bess)* We have a queen.

N1 No, we need a *fairy* queen.

N3   As you wish. *(gets some fairy wings and puts them on the sleeping queen—she will need to cooperate!)*

Oberon   *(to Puck)* I know a bank where the wild thyme blows; there sleeps Titania where the violet grows.

N3   *(sarcastically to N2)* There sleeps Queen Bess, so plug your nose!

Oberon   With the juice of this I'll streak her eyes
and make her full of hateful fantasies. *(takes a deep whiff of the giant pomander and then lurks behind the queen)*
> What thou seest when thou dost wake,
> do it for thy true love take,
> love and languish for its sake.
> be it ounce or cat or bear,
> pard or boar with bristled hair.
> When thou wak'st, it is thy dear.
> Wake when some *vile* thing is near. *(exits)*

Puck   That looks like fun. *(pulls out another flower)* I think I will try it on... *(looking around, then looks at narrators)*

N1   We're not sleeping—won't work.

Puck   *(looking around and going into the audience—again singing to tune of "It's a Hard Knock Life")*
> Through the theater have I gone,
> but a snoozer found I none,
> on whose eyes I might approve
> this flower's force in stirring love.

(finds Lymetrius, who is asleep in first row of audience)
> Night and silence! Who is here?
> Weeds of [spandex] he doth wear!

[or "yellow" or whatever he is wearing]
(rubs flower on his face)
> When thou wak'st, let love forbid,
> sleep his seat on thy eyelid.

(returns to stage)
> So awake when I am gone,
> for I must now to Al-anon! *(exits)*

N2   Al-anon?

N3 She must mean Alderaan. Er, Oberon. Look, here comes the blonde. . . er, brunette.

(enter Helena, out of breath)

Helena Oh, I am out of breath in this fond chase.
Where is Lymetrius and his cute little face?
Happy is Hermia, wheresoe'er *she* rests,
for *she* hath blessed and attractive. . .

(holds hands up in front of chest and looks down at them—then shakes her head)

no, wait, that's wrong. . .
Happy is Hermia, wheresoe'er she *lies*,
for she hath blessed and attractive thighs? Eyes!

(notices Lymetrius sleeping in the audience and goes to him)

But who is here? Lymetrius on the ground?
Dead, or asleep? *(poking him)*
I see no blood, no wound.
Lymetrius, if you live, good sir, awake!

Lymetrius *(waking and leaping onto stage)*
And run through fire I will for thy sweet sake!
Transparent Helena, nature shows art,
that through thy bosom makes me see thy heart.

(Helena gasps and crosses her arms over her chest. Hermia enters wearing a frame pack full of gear and holding a loaded marshmallow stick.)

Hermia *(yelling)* Demander? Where are you, my dear?

Lymetrius O Helen, goddess, nymph, perfect, divine!
To what, my love, shall I compare thine eyne?

Hermia Demander, what are you doing? *(takes off pack)* We were just about to roast marshmallows!

Lymetrius No, not marshmallows! It's *Helen* that I love.
Who would not change a pigeon for a dove?

Hermia A pigeon? *(to Helen)* You *stole* my Demander?

Helena *Your* Demander? That's *my* Lymetrius.

Hermia *(grabbing on to Lymetrius)* Demander, whereto tends all this?

Lymetrius Hang off, thou cat, thou burr! Vile thing, let loose!

Hermia *(to Helen)* O me! You juggler! You cankerblossom, You thief of love! What, have you come by night and stol'n my love's heart from him?

Helena Stolen? You're the one who just pranced in here with your plump little marshmallows and tried to burgle my boyfriend.

Hermia *(advancing on Helena, who is trying to stay safe behind Lymetrius)* I demand Demander, you dandelion, you noxious weed you! *(grabs Lymetrius, who shoves her to the ground and takes the bag of marshmallows—then he joins N1 to watch the fight)*

Helena Noxious weed? Ay, so *that* way goes the game. *(shoving Hermia)* You Canadian Thistle, wooly mullen, common *tea*sel!

Lymetrius *(to N1)* This is getting good. *(handing him a marshmallow like they are at the movies)* Excellent casting.

N1 Thanks.

Hermia You poison hemlock, perennial sowthistle, bulbous bluegrass! *(jabbing toward her with a loaded marshmallow stick)*

Helena *(picks up frame pack and uses it as a shield)* Oh yeah? You leafy spurge, onionweed, hairy willow-herb. . . *(slaps at her, girlishly)*

Hermia Ragwort, houndstongue, medusahead! *(pulls marshmallow off stick and throws it at her)*

N3 *(has gone behind Hermia and catches it)* Okay, enough horticulture. You're actors, not botanists!

N1 Could you just get on with the mud wrestling part?

Helena *(stops fighting)* Umm, we're not doing that!

Hermia You're sick! I nor longer stay in your curst company. *(She leaves.)*

Helena Me neither. *My* legs are *longer*, though, to run away! *(runs off)*

Lymetrius I guess this means my camping trip is over. *(gathers gear and leaves—N3 horks the marshmallows)*

(Captain Undergarments returns, oblivious to the audience, rehearsing a scene.)

N2 What is he doing?

CU/Bottom *(to himself)* Thisby, the flowers of odious savors sweet.

N3 Odorous!

CU/Bottom Odors savors sweet; so hath thy breath, my dearest Thisby dear...

N2 He thinks he's Pyramus. I didn't think we were doing that scene.

N3 We're not.

(Puck enters, laughing)

Puck What hempen, Fruit of the Loom-wearing, superhero have we swaggering here, so near the cradle of the Fairy Queen?

(lights go out, spotlighted custodian arrives, goes downstage, turns around and leans over to expose a fake butt-crack in the spotlight)

CU/Bottom *(looking toward butt)* Sweet moon, I thank thee for thy sunny beams; *(lights go back on, custodian gets up and leaves, CU looks at stage lights)* I thank thee moon for shining now so bright...

Puck A stranger Pyramus than e'er played here! I will make an even bigger fool of him!

CU/Bottom I see a voice. Now will I to the chink. *(Puck holds out her hand, and he looks through it—she slips her hand away and places a donkey head or ears on him—he remains focused on his lines.)* To spy an' I can hear my Thisby's face. *(approaches narrators as he looks around for Thisby)* Thisby? *(thinks N1 is Thisby and reaches out toward him)* If I were fair, Thisby, I were only thine. *(gets closer)*

(Narrators freak out and yell.)

N2 Oh monstrous! O strange!

N1 Under-donkey is after us!

N3 Run away!

(Narrators run away.)

To Do or NOT to Do. . .

CU/Bottom Why do they run away? I see their knavery. This is to make an ass of me, to fright me, if they could. I will walk up and down here, and I will sing, that they shall hear I am *not* afraid. Tra-la-la!
> The ouzel cock so black of hue,
> with orange-tawny bill,
> The throstle with his note so true,
> the wren with little quill.

(Queen Elizabeth stretches and wakes.)
Queen What *angel* wakes me from my flowery bed?
> I pray thee, gentle mortal, sing again.
> Mine ear is much enamored of thy note;

(gets up, looks curiously at her wings, and advances toward Bottom)
> so is mine eye *enthralled* to thy shape;

(touching his ears)
> on the first sound and view, I swear, I *love* thee.

CU/Bottom Methinks, mistress, you should have little reason for that. And yet, to say the truth, reason and love keep little company together nowadays.

Queen Thou art as *wise* as thou art beautiful.

CU/Bottom Thanks.

Queen *(petting his ears)* Wouldst thou like something to eat? Some purple grapes, green figs, or mulberries?

CU/Bottom Well, I kind of filled up on haggis backstage, but truly I could do with a peck of provender or some good dried oats.

Queen Come, I'll lead you to my bower. . .

CU/Bottom What's a bower? Is that like a pantry?

(Queen leads CU/Bottom backstage, still playing with his ears.)
Queen *(as they exit)* I'll stick musk roses in thy sleek smooth head, and kiss thy fair large ears, my gentle joy.

CU/Bottom I *could* eat musk roses. Ooh—that tickles.

(Oberon enters from the other side)
Oberon I wonder if Titania be awaked; then what it was that next came in her eye, which she must dote on in extremity.

(Puck returns)

Oberon How now, mad spirit?

Puck *(laughing hysterically)* My mistress with a monster is in love! Or rather, she's in love with a donkey in briefs. Lord, what fools these mortals be!

Oberon This falls out better than *I* could devise. *(The queen returns guiding Bottom.)* Hush, here they come. We are invisible. *(Oberon and Puck pretend to be invisible—N3 enters and joins them.)*

CU/Bottom Are we almost there yet?

Queen *(shoves him down)* Come, sit thee down upon this flowery bed, while *I* thy amiable cheeks do coy. *(reaches toward his back side)*

N3 Not *those* cheeks!

(Queen scratches his face, which he obviously enjoys.)

CU/Bottom Aaah, scratch again, for methinks I am marvelous hairy about the face. *(She does, and he shakes all over with enjoyment.)*

Queen Wilt thou hear some music, my sweet love?

CU/Bottom I have a reasonable good ear in music. *(yawning)* But right now I have an exposition of sleep come upon me. *(falls asleep)*

Queen Sleep thou, and I will wind thee in my arms. *(puts her arm around him and goes to sleep)*

(Puck and Oberon are laughing conspiratorially—N2 returns and sees the queen hugging the diaper donkey.)

N2 *(looking at the lovers)* This is just wrong!

(Oberon, Puck and N3 break out in laughter.)

N2 *(to Oberon)* This is *thy* negligence. You better fix this, or she will have us all beheaded!

Oberon Yeah, I have been a little mean to her lately. Her dotage now I do begin to pity. I'll undo this spell. *(goes over to her)*

N3 Wait! *(pulls out camera)* Let me get a picture first. *(takes picture)*

To Do or NOT to Do...

Oberon *(leaning over queen and squeezing an herb)* Be as thou wast *want* to be; see as thou wast *want* to see. Now, wake you, holy rancid queen. *(goes over to inhale from the pomander)*

Queen *(waking)* My people, what visions have I seen! Methought I was enamored of an a...

Puck *(interrupting and pointing at donkey)* There lies your love!

Queen *(screaming in repulsion)* Ahhh! How came this thing to pass?

CU/Bottom *(fart sound and he wakes up)* I have gas.

Queen O, how mine eyes do loathe his visage now! *(moving away and pointing)* Off with his head!

Puck Yes, your majesty. *(pulls on CU/Bottom's head, but it won't come off—finally pulls hard enough and donkey head goes flying while Puck falls backwards)*

CU/Bottom Ouch! My head hurts. *(standing, looking around, then speaking to audience)* I have had a most *rare* vision, or a *dream*. Methought I *was*—there is no man can tell what... *(feeling head)* methought I *had*...man is but an ass if he go around to expound *this* dream! It shall be written down! I will write a ballet *(rhymes with mallet)* of this dream, and then I shall sing it! Tra-la-la! *(pulls up undies and gives himself a wedgie, then flies off)*

N3 *(watching him go)* Au contraire, monsieur *(mon sewer)* derriere...

N2 or we'll hang you by your underwear. Thank goodness that's over.

Oberon Come, my queen, let's get you some deodorant and perhaps update your cosmetics. *(inhales from the pomander and pretends to hold his breath before he escorts her out)*

Queen My cosmetics? Why am I wearing wings? *(They leave.)*

Puck *(singing)* Now we fairies all must go;
we've done our damage to this show.
I am sent with broom, in hand,
to sweep this filth to La La Land.

Da da da da da! *(exits)*

(N1 returns)

N1 Good morrow, friends! I took care of that girl problem. I told them *I* could be Demander, and now we are all going on a double date to the [Rainbow Slide] after the show. So, where were we? *[Fill in your own special local place.]*

N3 Well, let's see. . . we've done the Greek play, the Roman orifice play, the twin romance play, the Scottish play with a bloodthirsty woman who was last seen in the ladies' room, the fairy play with the annoying character who sweeps and sings, and plenty of word play. So that still leaves the jelly play, the Danish play, and some dueling.

N1 You mean conspiracy, betrayal, murder, and teen romance.

N2 And don't we still have to honor the queen?

N1 Oh, right. *(Googling)* So, this next play is about a dad who has three daughters, one good and two bad. King Lear, king of unspecified ancient Britain, is aged and choleric (as opposed to melancholic or phlegmatic), which means he is overbearing, moody, and prone to bouts of anger and violence.

N3 *(under his breath to N2)* Like our director.

N2 *(elbows him)* Shh! Here come the castles.

(Three castles enter: a regular castle, a beach castle, and a ski castle. Best to make these out of cardboard so the daughters can carry them in.)

N1 King Lear is determined to divide his kingdom between his three daughters, Goneril, Regan, and Cordelia, according to the depth of their devotion and professed love for him. Be forewarned: there may be some more bodies to scrape up at the end of this one.

N2 And here they are.

(King Lear, Goneril, Regan, and Cordelia appear.)

Lear Daughters, whoever loves me most gets all my land and wealth, for I am tired and ready to retire. Who wants a big, fat dowry? Tell me, my daughters, which of you doth love me the most, that I my largest bounty may extend? Goneril, my eldest born—and with the ugliest name—speak first.

Goneril *(dramatically)*
        Sir, I love you more than can wield the matter;
        Dearer than eyesight, space, and liberty;
        beyond what can be valued, rich or rare;
        No less than life with grace, health, beauty, honor;
        As much as child e'er lov'd, or father found;
        A love that makes breath poor and speech unable;
        Beyond all manner of so much I love you.
(gives a false smile and winks at the audience)

Regan *(under her breath)* Brown noser. *(then smiling at her daddy)*

Cordelia *(aside)* What shall Cordelia speak? Love, and be silent.

Lear Well then, you shall have my shadowy forests, wide-skirted meads, lake-front property, the family castle, and the down-town shopping mall, including [Dillards and Starbucks.] *[replace with your own local favorites]*

Goneril *(aside)* Yes! *(then goes back to pretending to be sweet)*

Regan *(annoyed and jealous)* Awww!

Lear What say you, second daughter, Regan?

Regan *(sickly sweet)* Father, I am made of that same metal as my sister, and you should prize *me* as worthy. Only *I* love you more than *all* the senses combined—more than eyesight, ear-hearing, nose-smelling, mouth-tasting, *and* finger-feeling. I love you more than haggis and mutton, more than my *own* belly-button! Oh boy, do I love you! Can I have the beach vacation castle? Puh-lease? *(batting her eyes)*

Cordelia *(aside)* I am sure *my* love's more richer than a *false* tongue. But *I'll* not play this game.

Lear *(to Regan)* Of course, my dear Regan, it's all yours. Plus as much of this fair kingdom as bestowed upon your loving sister, Goneril.

Regan Woo-hoo! *(high-fives Goneril)*

Cordelia Well really, I love him most and am the most devoted daughter; but I am not going to say that, because it would seem insincere and false.

Lear And now, my third daughter, Cordelia, what say you?

Cordelia Nothing, my lord.

Lear Nothing?

Cordelia Nothing.

Lear Nothing will come of nothing. Speak again.

Cordelia Unhappy that I am, I cannot heave my heart into my mouth. I love your majesty according to my bond; no more nor less.

Lear How, how, Cordelia! Mend your speech a little, lest you may mar your fortunes.

Cordelia My father, you have begot me, bred me, lov'd me. I return those duties back as are right fit, obey you, love you and most honor you.

Lear No words of flattery for your dear old daddery?

Cordelia I only say what I feel, nothing more.

Lear Well, too bad. Let it be so. Thy *truth* then be thy dower, and good luck finding yourself a husband without a dowry. Here I disclaim all my paternal care, and as a stranger to my heart and me hold thee from this forever. My two devoted daughters' dowers shall digest the third!

N2 Uhh! That's not fair!

Lear *(violently, toward N2)* Come not between the dragon and his wrath! I lov'd her most! *(to Cordelia)* Get thee hence, and avoid my sight! Your sisters shall have your share.

Cordelia It's okay. I don't really like the beach anyway. I'll just herd sheep or something for a living. Maybe I'll find someone who loves me for my honesty, civility, and scrupulous virtues. I think I'll go to France. *(turns toward sisters)* Sisters, I know what you are and am too polite to call your faults as they are named. Use well our father; to your *professed* devotion I commit him, but alas I would prefer him to a better place. Take care of him as I would have. He likes mutton pie, poached pigeons with gooseberries, and green cheese; but don't give him lentils or let him drink sack before breakfast. So farewell to you both.

(Goneril and Regan sneer at her and wave good riddance as Cordelia leaves.)

Goneril Bye bye, daddy's little ex-pet!

Regan *(sarcastically)* We'll take care of the old coot. Good riddance!

Goneril Yes! That means we can split the ski-castle in the Highlands.

Lear So, devoted daughters, now that you have all my castles, I'll be taking turns visiting you with my 100 men. Make sure you have the beds made and plenty of food.

Goneril Yeah, right, Dad. Whatever you say.

Regan Let's go move into our castles and redecorate. I'm ordering new tapestries and lentils ASAP!

(Regan and Goneril exit, making redecorating plans as they go.)

Lear Somehow, I think I may have made the wrong decision. Those two were brats from birth. How could I be so blind? I feel like poking out somebody's eyes, to symbolize how blind I have been.

N3 Actually, you don't get to do any eye popping. One of the other characters gets to do that.

Lear Rats. Well, my men and I are tired and hungry. Let's see what Goneril has for dinner.

(Goneril and Regan are "in" their castles, or behind them rather—Lear goes and knocks on Goneril's door. He could have 100 little green army men attached behind him.)

Lear This is weird, knocking on my own castle door. Goneril, it's your father, the king. My 100 men and I are here for dinner, just like I said we would be.

Goneril *(from inside)* Go away! I'm not feeding you and your 100 reeking men. I'm busy getting rid of all your old clothes and stinky cheese. Go to Regan's castle.

Lear Come, men. Let's go to the beach castle.

(Lear drags his men to the other castle, where Regan is seen shutting the window when she sees him coming—he knocks on her door.)

Lear Regan, it's your father, the king. I'm hungry and tired and so are my 100 men. We are here for dinner and a good night's sleep, just like I said we would be.

Regan *(disguising her voice)* Nobody's home!

Lear Huh, nobody's home. Come men, let's try the ski castle in the Highlands. *(He drags his men to the ski castle façade and knocks.)* Daughter, it's your father, here for breakfast. *(tries to open the door)* They locked me out of the ski castle! Those two ungrateful little. . . I feel like popping somebody's eye out!

N3 Again, you don't get to do that. We had to abbreviate this play, and that deed belongs to a character who is not in our version.

Lear Who says? I'm the king, and I'm choleric! I'll pop out an eye if I want to! *(grabs N3 and pretends to pop out his eye)* Out, vile jelly!

N3 Ouch! My eye! *(Fake eyeball flies out.)* Hey—you're not following the script!

Lear What script? Where is my *nice* daughter, Cordelia? I *need* her.

N2 *(looking at eyeball)* Gross. *(asks audience)* Does anybody have a tissue? *(gets one from an audience member and then carefully picks up the eyeball and hands it to N3—then she digs through the prop trunk and finds an eye patch and gives it to him)*

N1 Well, and to make matters worse, you are about to be invaded by France.

Lear Ahh! I feel like popping out another eye!

N3 Restrain him! *(protecting his other eye)*

(N1 grabs Lear and pushes him onto a chair—N2 ties him up so he can't move.)

Lear I need my dear Cordelia. I have wronged her. *(weeps)*

N2 It's about time he figured that out.

(enter Cordelia)
Cordelia Here I am, father. I'll take care of you. By the way, the King of France married me—he loves me for my honesty. You don't look so good. Sir, do you know me?

Lear *(looks up at her, confused)* You are a spirit, I know. My one *good* daughter is gone. I sent her away. I am a very foolish old man. Is this lady really my child, Cordelia?

Cordelia I am.

Lear You came back to me?

Cordelia Of course, father. That's what decent daughters do. I'll even forgive you, if you let me have the ski castle.

Lear It's all yours! *(They hug.)*

N2 Aww. I know what you're all thinking: yay! A happy reunion! Sorry. As is typical for a Shakespearean tragedy, things go from worse to worse.

N1 Goneril and Regan are really and *truly* evil. They deceive and betray their father in their lust for power, and then they go after each *other*. Goneril plots to have her own husband murdered so she can take up with another man. Regan has also made plans of betrothal to the *same* man, so they become insanely jealous of each other. Eventually, Goneril poisons her sister and then stabs herself to avoid imprisonment.

(Goneril and Regan mime the poisoning and stabbing as the narrator talks—perhaps Goneril delivers a bowl of poisoned pudding to Regan, who eats it and dies dramatically, and then Goneril trips and falls on her sword on her way home.)

N2 But that's not all. . .

N3 Oh no, that's not all. . .

N2 Sweet and innocent Cordelia is captured and hung, by order of her sisters' boyfriend.

(N3 goes behind Cordelia and holds up a pretend rope; Cordelia grabs her neck, looks at N2 in dismay, and dies.)

Lear *(yelling)* Noooo! *(stabs N3, and then kneels behind Cordelia)* O, you are men of stones! Had I your tongues and eyes, I'd use them so that heaven's vault should crack. She's gone forever. She's dead as. . . *(touching her)* dirt. Lend me a looking glass. If that her breath will stain the stone, why, then she lives. *(holds a mirror up to her mouth—narrators shake their heads—Lear grabs a feather and holds it in front of her mouth)* If this feather stirs. . . it is a chance which does redeem all sorrows that ever I have felt. *(narrators shake their heads again and Lear realizes she is gone—looks out at audience)* Bring out the automated external defibrillator!

(Paramedic enters with an AED.)

N1   Can't use that—it hasn't been invented yet. Sorry.

(Paramedic leaves.)

Lear   A plague upon you, murderers, traitors all! I might have saved her; now she's gone forever! Cordelia, Cordelia! Stay a little. Ha! *(leans over her closely)* What is it thou sayst? *(looks at audience again)* Her voice was ever soft, gentle, and low, an excellent thing in a woman. *(looking at her)* I killed the slave that was a-hanging thee.

N3   *(still on the ground)* 'Tis true, he did.

Lear   *(to Cordelia)* Why should a dog, a horse, a rat have life, and thou no breath at all? Thou'lt come no more. Never, never, never, never, never! *(to N3)* Look! Her lips!

(Narrators shake their heads.)

Lear   *(despairingly)* Ohhhhhh. *(He dies.)*

N3   He is gone, indeed.

N1   *(calling backstage)* Clean up on aisle three!

N2   Have a little respect, will ya?

N1   Sorry, time's a wasting, and we must needs move on.

(Lear cast stands and bows, then clears castles off stage—N1 can take a little break here and return later—should play ghost/Vader voice from backstage—N2 exits to prep for Ophelia.)

N3   'Tis true. Bring on the next tragedy. And how about a little lute music, to lighten the mood!

(Lute player enters and makes Renaissance music while scene is being changed—after set is cleared, Hamlet arrives, all in black.)

Hamlet *(Lute player strikes a chord, and Hamlet starts singing a simple tune.)*
> My dad was murdered and my mom married my uncle;
> I'll sing that again cause nothing rhymes with uncle;
> My dad was murdered and my mom married my uncle;
> And now I'm going crazy.

(Gertrude enters.)

Gertrude Good Hamlet, cast thy nighted color off. Thou knowest 'tis common, all that lives must die, passing through nature to eternity.

Hamlet Ay, madam, it *is* common, though not customary for one's *mother* to marry one's *uncle* before one's *father* is even cold in the ground.

(Claudius enters.)

Claudius 'Tis sweet and commendable in your nature, Hamlet, to give these mourning duties to your father. But you must know *your* father lost a father, that father lost, lost his; likewise the father before that lost *his* father, etcetera, etcetera. What's the big deal?

Hamlet I would *rather* I had lost an *uncle*.

Gertrude Uhh! Hamlet! Don't talk to the king that way!

Hamlet He's no king to me.

Claudius *Come*, my queen. I think your son, my nephew, needs some space.

(Claudius and Gertrude leave.)

Hamlet *(mocking) Come* my queen. O *Mother*, how could you? Father was so excellent a king, and so loving to my mother. The funeral baked meats did coldly furnish forth the marriage tables. A *beast* would have mourned longer! O, what am I going to do?

Ghost voice *(in a Ghost Vader voice)* Avenge me!

Hamlet Father?

Ghost voice Yes, I am your father. Your uncle poured poison in my ear! Avenge me!

Hamlet But father, that would be wrong!

Ghost voice It is useless to resist. Join the dark side! Avenge me!

Hamlet Okay! I *will*, father, I *will!* I *will* avenge you!

(Ophelia enters.)

Ophelia Who are you talking to? I mean, to *whom* are you talking? You seem a little moody lately. Are we still going out? Hamlet? I thought you *loved* me.

Hamlet What's love? Don't ask my *mother*. Surely *she* doesn't know. How do I know you won't turn out like my *mother?*

Ophelia Well, you don't even *have* a brother.

Hamlet And if I *had? (sees her playing with trinkets)* What are *those? (looking at assorted tokens around Ophelia's neck—they could be large and random)*

Ophelia O, Hamlet. You know right well you gave me these tokens of love, and with them words of so sweet breath composed as made the things more rich. Have I been deceived?

Hamlet We have *all* been thus deceived. Get thee to a nunnery! Why wouldst thou be a *breeder* of sinners? It were better *my* mother had not borne *me*. Be thou as chaste as ice, as pure as snow. Ay, get thee to a nunnery, and quickly, too!

Ophelia *(aside, as she prepares to leave)* O, help him, you sweet heavens! What a noble mind is here o'erthrown!—And *I*, of ladies most deject and wretched, now see that noble and most sovereign reason like sweet bells jangled, out of tune and harsh. I wonder what he does next! Let us *spy* on him! *(goes to stage side to watch, and motions for N3 to join her—Hamlet should be alone on stage)*

Hamlet To *be*, or *not* to be: *that* is the question:
 Whether 'tis nobler in the mind to *suffer*
 the slings and arrows of outrageous *fortune*,
 or to take arms against a sea of troubles,
 and by opposing *end* them? To die: to sleep
 no more, and by a *sleep* to say we end
 the heart-ache. To die, to sleep—
 perchance to *dream!* Ay, there's the rub;

for in that sleep of death, what dreams may come?
But that *dread* of something *after* death
puzzles the will
and makes us rather *bear* those ills we have
than fly to *others* that we know *not* of.
Thus, *conscience* does make *cowards* of us all.
(yelling) Ophelia, I can still see you!
(goes over to the curtain, and she comes out)
But *who* is this behind the curtain? A *rat?*
(stabs curtain)

(N3 can conveniently become Polonius.)

N3/Polonius Dohhhhh! To thy own self be true! Brevity is the soul of wit! I am slain!

Ophelia You killed my father! *(They drag N3/Polonius downstage.)*

Hamlet Sorry, I thought that was my *uncle* lurking behind the curtain. I didn't know it was the fishmonger. It was an *accident.*

(Gertrude returns.)

Gertrude *(to Hamlet)* What hast thou done? O, what a rash and bloody deed is this!

Hamlet Almost as bad, good *Mother,* as kill a king and marry with his *brother.*

Gertrude You don't have any proof of that.

Hamlet Do too; Dad told me. He was there. For shame, Mother!

Gertrude O, speak to me no more! These words like daggers enter my ears. *(holding her ears)* No more!

Hamlet *(sarcastically)* You mean poison, poison in the ear.

Gertrude *(sits still holding ears)* I'm not listening.

Ophelia You killed my father. *(drags Polonius' body to one side of stage—Hamlet helps her if necessary)*

Hamlet Now we are both fatherless. *(goes across stage and plays with a skull)*

Ophelia *(covering her father with plants, flowers, rocks, etc. while singing an eerie tune, perhaps accompanied by lute player)*

He is dead and gone; he is dead and gone;
at his head a green-grass turf, at his heels a stone.

Polonius *(sitting up and echoing)* I am dead and gone. *(back down)*

Ophelia *(to audience)* Pray you, mark.
(singing again)
White his shroud as the mountain snow;
larded with sweet flowers. . . *(fading out)*
now 'tis time to say goodbye
to my dead sweet father. . .

Polonius *(echoing)* To your dead meat father.

(Claudius enters.)

Claudius *(to Gertrude)* What's wrong with her? What's wrong with you? What's wrong with him? Where's Polonius?

Gertrude *(still holding ears)* I'm not listening. I'm not listening.

Hamlet *(holding up skull and examining it)* At supper.

Ophelia *(singing)* His beard was white as snow,
and will not come again;
no, no, he is gone
and will not come again.

Polonius *(echoing)* And will not come again.

Claudius At supper? Where?

Hamlet *(pointing)* Not where he *eats*, but where he is *eaten*. A man may *fish* with the *worm* that hath *eat* of a king, and *eat* of the fish that hath *fed* of the worm.

Claudius Hamlet, this is murder.

Hamlet O, know *you* something of murder? *(grabs his crown and puts it on the ground)* O look, a sleeping king. Let me just pour a little something special in his ear. *(mimes pouring something)* How convenient; he won't wake up!

Gertrude *(still holding ears)* I'm not listening. I'm not listening.

Claudius You shall pay for this.

Hamlet It was *meant* to be you.

(Laertes enters with a travel bag.)

Laertes Hey sis. I'm home for spring break. Hey, new king. Hey soon to be brother–in–law. *(goes to high-five Hamlet, who turns away and goes back to talking to the skull)* What did I miss?

Ophelia *(approaching Laertes and pretends to give him something, then visits others during her monologue)* There's rosemary, that's for remembrance; pray you, love, remember. And there is pansies; that's for thoughts. There's oregano; that's for spaghetti sauce. There's fennel for you, and columbines. There's rue for you, and here's some for me; you must wear your rue with a difference. I *would* give you some violets, but they withered all when my *father* died. *(resumes singing)*
    Fare you well, my father;
    all flaxen was his poll.
    No, no, he is gone;
    have mercy on his soul.

Polonius *(echoing)* Have mercy on my soul.

Laertes What happened to my sister? Who killed my father?

Claudius Hamlet and Hamlet.

Hamlet *(still obsessed with skull)* It was an *accident!*

Laertes From friend to foe then. I'll not be juggled with. To hell, allegiance! I shall be revenged most thoroughly for my father. Oh heat, dry up my brains! Tears seven times salt burn out the sense and virtue of mine eye! By heaven, thy madness shall be paid with weight till our scale turn the beam. *(going to Ophelia)* O rose of May! Dear maid, kind sister, sweet Ophelia! O heavens, is it possible a young maid's wits should be as mortal as an old man's life? Nature is fine in love, and where 'tis fine it sends precious instance of itself after the thing it loves.

Ophelia *(singing and wandering off into the audience)*
    They bore him barefaced on the bier;
    hey nonny nonny, hey nonny non—
    and in his grave rained many a tear,
    fare you well my dove.

Laertes And so have I a noble father lost, and a sister driven into desperate terms. . . But my revenge will come!

Polonius *(singing once more)* Yes, please do avenge me.

Claudius *(aside to Laertes)* I just happen to have this chalice of seriously deadly poison. Let's dip our swords in it. Then all you will have to do is barely scratch Hamlet, and he's a goner. *(They dip their swords and then Claudius puts the cup down near Gertrude, who hasn't been paying attention.)*

(Hamlet gets up and puts down skull, looking at it.)

Hamlet *(to Laertes)* That skull had a tongue in it and could sing once, just like your father.

(Claudius grabs Laertes hand.)

Claudius Come, Hamlet, come and take this hand from me.

(Laertes and Hamlet shake hands.)

Laertes Hello. My name is Laertes. You killed my father. Prepare to die. *(holds sword toward Hamlet)*

Hamlet Give me your pardon, sir. I have done you wrong. But in my defense, I didn't know it was your dad behind that curtain. I was mad with revenge, just like you are now. I completely understand. It was the *crazy* Hamlet, not the *real* Hamlet.

Laertes I know it was an accident, but IT WAS MY DAD! *(prepares to fight)*

Hamlet In that case, may I borrow your sword? *(takes Claudius' sword)*

Claudius Umm. . .

Laertes No, not that one!

Hamlet Why not—scared? *(flicks Laertes with the poisoned sword and scratches him on the arm)*

N3 *(returning or standing up and brushing off flowers)* A hit—a palpable hit!

N1 *(returning)* Strike one.

Laertes *(grabs his arm)* Oh no!

Hamlet Oh, come on! It's only a flesh wound. Here, scratch me back, and we'll call it even. *(runs his arm into Laertes sword and scratches himself)*

N1 Strike two.

Claudius *(sarcastically)* Way to go, Hamlet. Very clever.

To Do or NOT to Do...

Laertes Oh, Hamlet, I'm so sorry.

Hamlet What? You haven't even done anything. You're acting like I've been poisoned.

Laertes *(pointing to Claudius)* It's all *his* fault. He *made* me do it! *(falls)*

Hamlet You *tampered* with the blades? I've been *poisoned?*

Gertrude Ahh! All this killing is making me thirsty. *(grabs chalice and chugs)*

Claudius *(unconvincingly)* No, Gertrude, stop.

N3 Too late.

N1 Strike three.

Gertrude *(super-dramatic!)* The drink! The drink! I am poisoned. *(dies)*

Hamlet Mother?

Laertes Hamlet, in thee is not 30 seconds life. I am sorry I killed you. Seek your revenge—and quickly. *(dies)*

Hamlet 28, 27. O villainy! 25. Treachery! 23. Treason!

N3 And for what was the reason?

Hamlet *(going toward Claudius)* Hello. My name is Hamlet. 18. *(to audience)* Yes, like a small pig. 16. *(to Claudius)* You killed my father, my mother, my girlfriend's brother, and me. Prepare to get what's coming to you. *(to N1)* 12. Lock the door! Venom, do thy work. Give me the cup! 8.

(N1 and N3 detain Claudius while Hamlet stabs him with sword then pours the poison in his ear, mouth, and nose.)

Hamlet *(as he kills Claudius)* 5. For me, 4, for my father, 3, for my mother, 2, for my girlfriend's brother, 1, for my...

N1 Strike four. All right, Hamlet. That's enough. Your 30 seconds are up.

Hamlet I have gone into overtime! The potent poison quite o'ercrows my spirit. O, I die! The rest is silence. *(dies)*

N3/Pig *(whips out pig puppet)* So long, little piggy, my love. So sorry we didn't get a chance to go hog wild together.

N1 What are you doing?

N3/Pig   Can't a pig have some time to pine for her swine?

N1   Oh look, here comes Ophelia!

N3/Pig   Ooop! Gotta go! *(flings the puppet out of sight)*

(Ophelia enters, stepping over bodies.)

N1   A little late—play's over.   Besides, weren't you supposed to fall in a river and drown?

Ophelia   Yeah, well. . . I got to thinking about that. I'm *tired* of going down in history as the love-sick girlfriend who goes loony and throws flowers and can't even *swim*. I'd rather be strong, confident, and resilient. My *happiness* and my *future* shouldn't hinge on the actions of a *man*, even if he *is* cute. I've got my whole life ahead of me—I'm young and pretty, I can sing, *and* I am a talented herbologist. I could get a job as an apothecary and work on a cure for the plague. *(scratching herself)*

N3   I'll give you a clue: eradicate the fleas.

Ophelia   *(still scratching her head and other parts)*   The what?

(Lady Macbeth wanders in.)

N1   And *you're* still wandering around? You were supposed to die before intermission.

Lady Mac   Well, what is the point of *we* becoming king if I just kill myself? This whole Shakespearean suicide thing is just stupid—I want to see where life is going to take me. I know I made some egotistical, unethical, and disreputable choices, but I want a chance to redeem myself and make something of my life now that I'm unhampered by a husband. Besides, what's wrong with a woman having power? Do you have a problem with that?

N1   Uh, no.

Lady Mac   Besides, I can't get my hands clean.

N3   Have you tried soap?

Lady Mac   Uh, no.

N3   Well, we could do *Titus Andronicus* and just cut them off and put them in a pie.

Lady Mac   I'll go try soap. *(She exits.)*

To Do or NOT to Do...

N1 *(to the dead guys)* Alright, deceased—the Danish play is over. Rise up and exit. I'm getting tired of hauling off the dead.

(Hamlet, Laertes, Claudius, and Gertrude delay by taking a bow, then are shooed off by N1. Pig puppet/N3 runs after Hamlet.)

N3/Pig My little Hamlet is alive! Wait for me, Hammy.

N2 *(calling after pig puppet)* You know, a pig in lipstick is still a pig! *(N2 takes off her Ophelia garb, either in view of audience or behind a curtain, depending on what she is wearing.)* What do we have left?

N1 *(Googling)* Well, fortunately not *Titus Andronicus*—that one's too revolting even for us. We have definitely covered conspiracy, betrayal, and murder—but we have yet to combine them with teen romance and light-saber dueling.

N2 *(sighing)* Ahh! Finally! *Romeo and Juliet*. What do you mean "light-saber dueling?"

(Star Wars-ish music begins—or wandering minstrel could play it on the lute!)

N2 Oh no! You wouldn't! You'll ruin it!

N1 Nonsense, it'll be great—you just wait. We even have a prologue.

(could be done with a character playing "Yoda" or with a doll and overhead voice—should be downstage center)

Yoda-logue Households two, alike in dignity both
   Our scene we set, on Tatooine so bleak
   Mutiny from ancient grudge regrowth
   Unclean make civil hand and cheek
   Cast forth from fatal loins of foe
   Lovers young cross stars and life they take
   Jedi Knights no help to Han Solo
   Rebel Force beware or Empire shall break.

N2 What have you done to my favorite play?

N1 Sorry, just making sure we honor those requests! Would you like to be an Ewok?

N2 No thanks—I'd rather pretend this isn't happening.

(Abraham and Sampson arrive from two opposing sides in either Renaissance or Star Wars garb with light sabers—Sampson crosses in front, so his back is to audience—then they face each other.)

Abraham Do you bite your *thumb* at me, sir?

Sampson I do *bite* my thumb, sir.

Abraham But do you bite your thumb at *me*, sir?

Sampson Is the law on my side if I say ay?

Abraham No.

Sampson Well, in *that* case, I do not bite my *thumb* at you, sir; but I do bite my pinkie. *(bites pinkie in Abraham's direction)*

Abraham What does *that* mean?

Sampson Wouldn't *you* like to know!

Abraham Are you trying to start a fight, sir?

Sampson Apparently. *(They duel with sabers.)*

(Friar Obi enters.)

Obi   Part, fools! Put down your sabers! You know *not* what you do. Throw your mistempered weapons to the ground. This play is about *love*, not *war*. Hand over your weapons before somebody gets hurt.

(They give Friar Obi their weapons, disappointed.)

Sampson Aww! Love is a very apoplexy, mulled, death, sleepy, insensible, BORING. . . War is spritely, waking, audible, and much more exciting!

Abraham *(to Sampson)* Hey, I saw some blasters backstage.

Sampson Sweet! *(They exit—perhaps some blaster sounds are heard in the background after they leave.)*

N2   Thank you. Where's Romeo?

(N3, dressed like Luke Skywalker, returns with R2D2 or similar droid.)

N3   Hey look—this little medical droid fixed my eye.

N2   Romeo Skywalker?

N3   Or Luke Montague, I guess.

N1 *(patting him on the back)* Better you than me. I'm afraid of heights.

N2 Can we just cut to the balcony scene? I *love* the balcony scene. 'Tis but thy *name* that is my enemy. . .

(Droid makes beeping noises—holograph is being set up.)

N1 I think the little droid is trying to tell you something.

(Droid "projects" a holograph of Princess JuLeia—this can be accomplished with a spotlight and a fog machine pointed at JuLeia.)

N3 But soft, what light from yonder holograph breaks? Listen.

JuLeia *(as a holograph)* Help me, Friar Obi. My parents want me to marry Prince Paris, but he is a pompous space slug. My lips, my red and tender lips, instead prefer that guy I kissed at the party the other day. But he's a Montague! My only love has sprung from my only hate. O Romeo, Romeo, wherefore art thou, Romeo?

N3 Whoa! Who's that hot chick, R2? She's like part girl, part hamburger! I could order that!

(Holograph light goes off.)

N2 Oh brother.

JuLeia *(steps up onto balcony)* Yeah, speaking of *brother*, this just isn't gonna work. I'd just as soon kiss a Wookiee. Could you get me *Han* Romeo instead? At least *we're* not related.

N3 You're my sister? My bad. I'll go get Han Romeo from the cantina. *(exits and sends forth Han Romeo)*

JuLeia Thank you.

Han Romeo *(seeing JuLeia, who has her hand on her hip, then talking to audience)*
    It is my lady, O, it is my love!
    See how she leans her cheek upon her hand?
    O, that I were a *glove* upon that hand,
    that I might touch that *cheek!*

JuLeia Ay me! *(moves her hand to her face cheek!)*

Han Romeo *(to audience)* She speaks! *(to JuLeia)*

O, speak again, bright angel,
for thou art as glorious to this night,
being o'er my head,
as is a winged Geonosian of the Outer Rim,
unto the white-upturned wondering eyes
of mortals that fall back to gaze on him,
when he bestrides the lazy puffing clouds
and sails upon the bosom of the air.

N1 *(nudging N3, laughing)* Bosom?

N2 Grow up. Shhh!

JuLeia *(talking to herself, mainly)* Han Romeo?
Is that you, Han Romeo?
Deny thy father and refuse thy name!
'Tis but thy *name* that is my enemy;
thou art *thyself*, though, not a Montague.
What's Montague? It is nor hand, nor foot,
nor arm, nor face, nor nose, nor any *other* part
belonging to a man.

(N1 and N3 bust out in laughter and are shushed by N2.)
O, be some *other* name!
What's *in* a name? That which we call a rose
by any *other* name would smell as sweet;
so Han Romeo would, were he not Han Romeo called.

Han Romeo By a name, I know *not* how to tell thee who I am. Call me whatever you like. How do I get up there?

JuLeia I don't know—try using the force!

(He tries levitating, but fails.)

N3 You're gonna have to climb.

(Romeo climbs up—perhaps with assistance of narrators.)

Han Romeo *(panting after struggling up the wall)* With love's light wings did I o'erperch these walls.

JuLeia If my kinsmen see thee, they will murder thee.

Han Romeo My life were better ended by their hate than death prorogued, wanting of thy love.

JuLeia If thou *dost* love, pronounce it faithfully.

Han Romeo Lady, by yonder blessed moon of Endor, I vow. . .

To Do or NOT to Do...

JuLeia O, swear *not* by the *moon*, the inconstant *moon,* that monthly changes in her circled *orb.*

Han Romeo Then by the planet Alderaan, Shining Star of the Core Worlds. . .

JuLeia No, not by *Alderaan*—that gets destroyed by the *Death Star.*

N3 *(to N1)* But it would be a great use of foreshadowing.

N1 *(calling up to JuLeia)* How about Tatooine?

JuLeia *(to N1)* No, too hot and dry and full of Womp Rats.

Han Romeo Bespin?

JuLeia A gas giant? O, do not swear at all. Or if thou *wilt,* swear by thy gracious *self,* and I'll believe thee.

(Wookiee sound is heard from behind.)

JuLeia *(calling to nurse)* Coming, nurse!

(another Wookiee sound)

JuLeia *(calling to nurse)* I'm just talking to the stars. Just a minute! *(to Romeo)* Sweet, good night! This bud of love may prove a beauteous flower when next we meet!

Han Romeo Huh? That's it?

N3 Suspense!

JuLeia What satisfaction canst thou have tonight?

Han Romeo The exchange of thy love's faithful vow for mine.

JuLeia I gave thee mine before thou didst request it.

(more Wookiee sounds)

JuLeia *(irritated)* Anon, I come, nurse! *(to Romeo)* My love is as deep as the sea; the more I give thee, the more I have, for *both* are infinite.

N2 *(looking up and sighing)* Ohh. Love metaphors.

N1 *(Googling)* Meta what?

JuLeia *(to N1)* Shhh! You're ruining my scene.

Han Romeo *(to JuLeia)* *Our* scene, you mean. O blessed night, I am afeard, being in night, this is all a dream.

JuLeia Dear Romeo, if thy love be honorable, thy purpose marriage, meet me at Friar Obi's tomorrow.

(Wookiee sounds and Wookiee arms come out and grab JuLeia)

JuLeia *(struggling against Wookiee arms)* Good night, my love. Parting is such sweet sorrow! *(pulled out of sight)*

(Romeo climbs down, very disappointed—N1 pats him on the back.)

N1 Tough break, man.

Han Romeo Friar Obi!

Obi Hey, Han Romeo. You're up early. *(gesturing to the sky)* The grey-eyed morn smiles on the frowning night, check'ring the eastern clouds with streaks of light.

N3 Nice morning metaphor; but get along with the plot!

Obi *(continuing)* Now, ere the sun advance his burning eye, the day to cheer and night's dank dew to dry.

N1 Ahem.

Obi *(to narrators)* Oh, sorry. *(to Romeo)* Benedicite, Romeo! Thy earliness doth assure me that something's up. How can I help you?

Han Romeo I want you to marry me this morning!

Obi *(coughing and sputtering)* Dude, no! Well, I *am* flattered; but you know very well that I am a man of the holy order and . . .

Han Romeo Uhh! No! Not marry *me!* I need you to perform the marriage rites between me and my *true* love!

Obi Okay, *that* I can do. Where's Rosaline?

Han Romeo No, *not* Rosaline. I have forgot *that* name.

Obi Jesmin Ackbar?

Han Romeo She flew off days ago! No, *JuLeia!*

Obi Who's JuLeia?

Han Romeo The girl I met, wooed, and exchanged vows with last night.

Obi Young people these days! *(calling)* Come in, JuLeia.

N3 And so, they were married.

Obi Latin, Latin, Latin—I now pronounce you. . . kissy kissy!

(They lean together for the kiss, but are interrupted by N1, who steps between them.)

N1　　But before they can make anything of it, Romeo accidentally kills JuLeia's cousin and is banished.

(Romeo can have a quick light-saber duel, killing N1 and then running off—JuLeia should run to the arms of the Wookiee nurse for comfort.)

JuLeia　*(sobbing)* Oh, nurse! My Han Romeo is banished!

(comforting Wookiee sounds)

Obi　　JuLeia *Capulet?* You just tricked me into marrying a Montague and a Capulet? Your parents will kill me! They'll kill you! You would be better off dead! Which makes me think of a clever plan to teach them a lesson and trick them into getting along.

N2　　Well, it's not all *that* clever. It backfires and pretty much ruins the ending. No Katniss Everdeen berry trick in *this* story—they're gonna have to actually die before their feuding families learn a lesson.

N3　　Who says we have to end it that way? This is *our* play. Let's leave the ending up to the viewer's discretion.

(JuLeia rejoins them.)

JuLeia　Besides, we *really* need to get back to fighting the Evil Empire. Let's go tell Han. *(JuLeia and Obi exit.)*

N3　　See you in space, sister!

Han Romeo　*(heard from backstage)* Sweet, hop into the Millennium Falcon, and let's take on the Dark Side!

(engine blasting and Wookiee sounds)

N2　　Well, that was interesting. I do like the evasive ending. It gives a girl hope.

N1　　*(getting up and looking at N2)* A new hope.

N2　　*(ignoring him)* I think that about wraps it up.

(Queen returns, looking much better.)

N3　　Well, look who has discovered 21st century cosmetics!

N2　　*(to audience)* Uh oh! We forgot to honor the queen. She'll have our heads!

Queen   I'm back for my Falstaff and for the play about me.

N3   Well, actually, the play is entitled *Henry VIII*, so it's mostly about your dad.

(A ridiculously royal-looking King Henry arrives, perhaps with wandering minstrel on electric guitar—Captain Undergarments could double as King Henry for added humor!)

Henry   *(loudly sings part or all of the familiar "Henry the 8th" song by Herman's Hermits)*

N3   *(cutting him off)* Hold it! Umm. . . That song isn't actually about the king.

Henry   It's not?

Queen   I should say not! My father never married the widow next door! Unless you count his *first* wife, Catherine of Aragon, who *was* his *brother's* widow—but *she* just lived down the hall.

N2   That plot sounds familiar.

N1   *(Googling)* Unfortunately, in 1613, a canon backfired during a production of *Henry VIII* and set the Globe on fire, ending the performance. *(looks at Henry)*

Henry   *(starts panicking, over-acting, and running around)* Ahh! I'm on fire! Ahh! *(runs around while everyone else remains calm)*

N3   *(looking at him and speaking without expression, perhaps with his lips rolled up over his teeth)* Stop, drop, and roll, Henery.

Henry   *(looks at N2, stops, drops, rolls, then gets back up)* Huh, never heard of that. Thanks, Fire Marshal (N3's name). *(exits)*

N2   *(hand on neck for protection)* But, we did manage to salvage the most important verse, which is all about Master Shakespeare's beloved queen. William produced a most brilliant and flattering prophesy about the infant princess.

N3   Who's doing it? *(to N1)* Get the red-haired baby.

(N1 tosses baby to N3.)

N3   This isn't my monologue.

N2   Oh brother. *(taking baby and stepping forward)* This royal infant, Elizabeth, promises upon this land a thousand, thousand blessings, which time shall bring to ripeness. Truth shall nurse her; holy and heavenly thoughts shall counsel her.

Queen   *(stepping in and taking the baby)* I shall be loved and feared; In my days every man shall eat in safety and sing the merry song of peace to all his neighbors. I shall be, to the happiness of England, an aged princess; and yet no day without a deed to crown it.

N1   *(taking baby)* But, she must die. . .

N3   *(taking baby)* She must!

N2   The saints must have her! *(takes the baby from N3 and puts it down)*

N3   A most unspotted lily shall she pass to the ground, and all the world shall mourn her.

Queen   I die?

N2   Of course you die. So sorry.

N3   But your memory lives on in the hearts of your people.

N1   Just be glad you die of old age. They say you died easily, like a ripe apple from a tree. *(mimes picking an apple and biting it)*

Queen   *(looking over N1's shoulder at iPhone)* At what age? What is the cause?

(N1 puts away iPhone.)
N1   I'm not telling you when! But they do think it was blood poisoning.

N3   So keep your ears covered!

N2   It was probably from all that lead-based make-up you were wearing!

Queen   Where's my Falstaff? *(tyrannically)* You promised me Falstaff!

N1   *(calling backstage)* Hey, guys! The queen demands her Falstaff!

(Han Romeo and Friar Obi enter.)

Han   What's a Falstaff?

Obi Oh rats! We thought you said *holograph!*

(Everyone protects their necks. N3 goes over to the queen and bows.)

N3 Umm, unfortunately, your royal highness, Sir Falstaff was too fat to time travel. You, apparently, are not. If it pleases you, you could enter the royal purple throne room and arrive back in your court just in time to see the Lord Chamberlain's men perform a play written especially for you all about the gluttonous knight.

Queen *(excited)* Did Master Shakespeare write about Sir Falstaff in love?

N3 He did, just like you requested.

Queen I command you take me there at once!

N1 *(calling backstage)* We need the purple porta-potty time machine!

(Captain Undergarments enters with the time machine.)

Captain U Tra la la! Sir Undergarments to the rescue!

N1 *(Googling)* Program it to the palace at Richmond, February 2, 1603.

(Queen checks out the purple porta-potty time machine and is pleased—pulls out toilet seat and puts it over her head, like a necklace.)

Queen *(rubbing her hand on the toilet seat)* How exquisite! How does it work?

Captain U *(escorting her)* You put your royal heinie in here, and when you are ready, you just push. . . this lever. It's really simple. Got it?

Queen Yes. It reminds me of my chamber pot. And my Falstaff will appear?

N3 Most definitely, your highness.

Captain U *(handing her a plunger)* Here, you might need this.

Queen *(caresses it and perhaps sticks it to her face)* What do I do with it?

N3 *(sarcastically)* Not that.

To Do or NOT to Do...

Queen *(to CU)* I am ready. *(gets in time machine and turns toward audience, brandishing plunger like a scepter)* My people, do whatever you like. I know I have the body of a frail and feeble woman, but I have the heart and stomach of a king. You may have a wiser prince sitting in this seat, but you never have had any who loves you better. *(closes the door and flushing sound is heard)*

N2 I might actually miss her. We should have sent her with some modern cosmetics. Might have prolonged her life.

N3 Nope, it's already 1603. She doesn't have much time anyway.

N1 Well, now that she's gone, and we all still have our heads, we can end this.

N2 Did we get everything on the list? What's the grand tally?

N1 *(looking at iPhone)* Let's see. . . over a dozen "ridiculius" Greek and Roman names,

N3 including several that sound like contagious diseases.

N1 21 deliberate acts of betrayal, five counts of conspiracy, two successful acts of revenge, 17 cold-blooded murders, over 300 deaths, if you count the nameless Plebeians who were starved and beaten by their ruthless ruler. . .

N3 *(raising arm)* We like pancakes! [We like pancakes!]

N1 and various random acts of violence.

N3 Yeah! My eye!

N2 Three sets of twins, *not* identical; three fairies with fluttery wings; a variety of tights and tunics, plus three boys in skirts!

N1 *(defensively)* Two of them were kilts!

N2 16 strong, resilient, non-subservient female characters.

N3 Did you count the nurse?

N2 17. Some of whom were bloodthirsty, yet powerful.
(Lady Macbeth enters)
Lady Mac Look! My hands came clean!

N1 One bar of soap.

N3 39 bowls of haggis consumed, half of them by a single actor.

N1 Five double love interests and nine romantic hook-ups.

N2 *(counts on her fingers and then glares at N1)* Eight.

N3 A whole menagerie of wildlife, including six rats, five dogs, two pigs, a gerbil and an ass.

(Captain Undergarments enters.)

Captain U *(patting stomach)* Boy, after all that haggis and roughage, I could use a good BM.

N2 *(annoyed)* Uh! That's enough!

Captain U What? Bacon and mayonnaise sandwich. It's even better than haggis!

(N3 whips out pig puppet.)

N3/Pig Did somebody say bacon? *(attacks CU)* Hi-yah! Take that, you freaky undergarments-wearing, not-really-a-superhero guy!

(N1 and N2 pull N3/Pig off CU.)

N2 *(consolingly)* It's okay, Piggy. He didn't mean *you*. He meant turkey bacon.

N3/Pig Oh. Can I borrow your lipstick?

N2 Sure. *(puts some on pig puppet)*

N3/Pig Thank you. I'm off to see my Hammy! *(N3 takes her backstage and returns.)*

N2 *(yelling after pig)* He's not even your species!

N1 *(looking at iPhone)* Whoa! 40 different body parts referenced! Well, one was only inferred, because nobody would say it.

N3 Did you get the twins' father's mole?

N1 41.

(Regan enters.)
Regan Did you get my bellybutton?

(Hermia enters)
Hermia Are goosebumps body parts?

(Sampson enters, holds up thumb, then bites pinkie.)

N1   45. We might have to do a recount.

N2   *(looking at CU, who is scratching himself)*   More immature allusions to gastrointestinal processes than many of us could stomach.

Captain U *(offers pill to N2)* Would you like a Pepto?

(N2, looking a bit ill, accepts it and pops it in her mouth.)

Obi   A subversive, Star Wars sub-plot!

(Han Romeo, Friar Obi, N1, and N3 high five each other—Wookie sounds are heard, and arms wave from backstage.)

N3   Thousands of omissions, hundreds of conversions, dozens of distortions, and plenty of perversions.

(Orsino enters, picks up a shoe, sniffs it, and holds it to his heart.)

N2   *(looking at him)* Case in point.

N1   So, what shall we call it?

N3   I know! Out, Vile Jelly-filled Donut! *(holding up Duncan's donut crown)*

N1   Like anyone would come to see that!

N2   Since it was all wrong, and we probably never should have done it, how about To Do, or NOT to Do?

N1   Or, Shakespeare! *(waving arms around)* Gone Astray!

N3   In 3D!

N1   It wasn't in 3D.

N3   Of course it was! *(throws a marshmallow at him)* We're always in 3D!

(Annie/Puck enters, singing.)

Puck   What about the epilogue, the epilogue? We have to have an epilogue!

N2   And an annoying character who sweeps and sings.

N1   Sure, we can do an epilogue. . .in the iambic tetrameter, or a variation thereof?

N2   Listen to you, poetry geek! Let's have all of our actors join us!

N1   I'll begin.

(Any remaining actors arrive discreetly—spotlight could travel to each one for his/her line—N1 goes downstage center—actors should try to "out-stage" each other for the finale! Some of these lines can be split to accommodate a cast larger than 21.)

N1	If we actors have offended
N3	'Twas our intention, 'twon't be mended
N2	You paid five bucks, what'd you expect?
Olivia	Kenneth Branaugh here to direct?
Coriolanus	Greeks and Romans; darn plebeians;
Friar Obi	Some Jedi Knights and Europeans;
Viola	Shoe inhalers, messed-up twins;
Lady Mac	Bloody hands and pudding skins;
Hermia	Marshmallows, F.O.U.S.'s;
Lymetrius	Some girls in very ugly dresses;
Lear	Ungrateful daughters, a popped-out eye;
Gertrude	A morbid, vengeful, crazy guy;
JuLeia	Romantic passions and a Wookiee;
Han Romeo	Language full of gobble-de gookie;
Regan	A purple potty time machine;
Oberon	That helped expel a stinky queen;
Puck	Fairy creatures and an ass;
Captain U	But now we have run out of gas.
Cordelia	It was all for your delight.
Queen	*(stepping out of potty)* We hope you liked it—so good...

Hamlet *(cutting off Queen)* You guys, I think we need a disclaimer.

N1   A what?

Hamlet   A *dis*claimer!

N3   Good idea. Disclaimer: The [insert the name of your theater group] in no way, shape, or form condones dying, killing, stealing, betraying, or the consumption of haggis for other than theatrical purposes.

Obi Only egos and self-images were damaged in the production of this play.

N2 No rights reserved, for this was certainly *all* wrong.

N1 No returns, exchanges, or refunds.

Queen We hope you liked it—so good night.

(We suggest "Henry the 8th" by Herman's Hermits during curtain call, then some Star Wars Cantina Music—if you are hosting an amateur, non-profit production!)

Katherine T. Dumont

To Do or NOT to Do: Shakespeare Gone Astray! (in 3D)

Written and directed by Katherine Tartaglia Dumont

Original Cast:

Narrator 1/MacBuff	Peter Herman
Narrator 2/Ophelia	Aspen Turner
Narrator 3/Boy/Weird Sisters/Polonius	Theodore Dumont
Annie/Puck/Jeweler	Zoe Hester
Han-Romeo/Timon/Butt Custodian	Harrison Daley
Friar Obi/Malvalentine/Laertes	Finn Tierney
JuLeia/Painter/Valeria	Nadia Herman
Captain Undergarments/Nick Bottom	Spencer Holmes
Hamlet/Apemantus	Seth Greer
Minstrel/Coriolanus/Sampson	Gio Dumont
Good Queen Bess/Titania	Chloe Burke
Greek Column 1/Regan/Abraham	Molly Morgan
Greek Column 2/Cordelia	Annalise Basch
Poet/Olivia	Bailey Ash
Lucilius/Banquo, etc./King Lear	Will Thomas
Ventidius/Sebastian/Oberon	Finnian T. Martin
Volumnia/Lady Mac	Kiera Wendell
Orsino/Lymetrius/Henry VIII	Axel Engel
Viola/Goneril	Emma Laurienti
Helena/Gertrude	Kassidy Glassman
Hermia/Claudius	Tori Armitage
Yoda-logue	Frank Dumont

Intermission: Renaissance Lute performed by Gio Dumont
Cover art by Nadia Herman

To Do or NOT to Do. . .

Fun with Pseudo-Shakespearean Insults
The actors loved these and thought you would, too!

Start with "thou," take a barb from each column, and bludgeon both friend and foe with creative curses!

bawdy	beef-witted	pig-bladder
churlish	clay-brained	coxcomb
fobbing	regurgitating	bellybutton
gleeking	flea-bitten	fish-bikini
gor-bellied	rump-fed	barnacle
frothy	half-witted	mutton-butt
spongy	milk-livered	bosom
venomed	onion-eyed	teenager
paunchy	dog-hearted	Wookiee-kisser
spleeny	toad-spotted	kidney-face
warped	haggis-skinned	meat-nugget
yeasty	adolescent	hugger-mugger
weedy	donut-shaped	pudding-breath
lumpish	snorting	entrails
puking	marrowless	slab of pork
reeky	bloody-handed	rat-sphincter
infectious	flatulent	marshmallow
bulbous	bean-fed	canker-blossom
greasy	odorous	Medusa-head
murky	phlegmatic	under-donkey
fleshy	eye-popping	pigeon-poo
rancid	tapioca	defibrillator
poached	jelly-filled	plebeian
soggy	Shakespearean	noodle-noggin

Body parts referenced:

flesh	eyes	nose
lips	eye lids	blood
bones	entrails	butt
tongue	heart	hair
bosom	arm	anus
liver	pinkie	hands
ear	back	mole
stomach	cheeks	neck
chin	brow	bill
lungs	face	marrow
tail	goatee	brain
toe	wings	mustache
mouth	head	finger
bellybutton	heels	thumb
breasts (inferred)	goosebumps	legs

To Do or NOT to Do...

Useful props by scene:

Intro
basket with suggestions (including green paper for *SHREK* and pod racer origami for *Star Wars*)
2 apples
Darth Vader mask
10 Shakespeare books
2 light sabers
mustache
droid
gerbil for CU
broom for Annie
Renaissance garb for N3, N1, and N2
throne for queen

Timon of Athens
10 bags of gold in basket
plate of food
two paintings—one should be a mockery of Timon in his pillowcase
gem
fake rock (wrapping duct tape around newspaper works—then nobody gets hurt!)

Coriolanus
sword and shield for Coriolanus
fake blood (backstage)
laundry basket for Valeria

Twelfth Night
shoe for Orsino
mustache and goatee for Malvalentine
inflatable whale for Viola
assorted sea critters for Sebastian
recorder for Malvalentine
wearable Valentine for Viola

Macbeth
bowls of haggis
cauldron with entrails
pig puppet or doll
rodent puppet or doll
witch dress and wig for N3
scarf and babies for Banquo
dog ears and nose
dagger for Macbeth
three other swords, one with blood on it
bagpipes
ghost sheet
donut crown for Duncan

A Midsummer Night's Dream
bag of marshmallows
frame pack with petticoat sticking out
flower for Puck
giant pomander (attach flowers and greenery to a wire ball 2-3
    feet in diameter)
wings for queen
ass head
fake butt for custodian
camera for N3

King Lear
portable castle, beach castle, ski castle (cardboard with windows
    on castle and beach castle so Goneril and Regan can peek
    out)
100 men on belt for King Lear
eyeball for N3
eye patch for N3
feather
handheld mirror
bowl of haggis

Hamlet
lute
rat for Hamlet

To Do or NOT to Do. . .

skull for Hamlet
flowers for Ophelia
chalice
two swords
pig puppet
beads on Ophelia
white beard for Polonius

R and J
two light sabers
fog machine
Yoda
Droid
Wookiee arms

Finale
purple porta-potty time machine
toilet seat
plunger
red-haired baby
pig puppet for N3
shoe for Orsino
marshmallow for N3

Notes:

To Do or NOT to Do...

ABOUT THE AUTHOR

Katherine Tartaglia Dumont is a secondary English teacher by trade and a writer by default. She started directing and writing plays for kids when her oldest son was five. (Somehow her troupe expanded and became teenagers, and now the actors are demanding more and more challenging parts!) Dumont majored in English and in Russian Studies at St. Olaf College and received an MA in Education from the University of CO in Boulder. She lives with her family in beautiful Estes Park, CO, the gateway to Rocky Mountain National Park, where she enjoys spending time on the trails. She runs the Soggy Noodle Children's Theatre, serves as teen librarian at the local library, and teaches classical/finger-style guitar on the side.

www.ingramcontent.com/pod-product-compliance
Lightning Source LLC
Chambersburg PA
CBHW061337040426
42444CB00011B/2960